# The IRA in Kerry
## 1916–1921

SINÉAD JOY graduated from University College Cork in History and Irish in 1996. Having completed a Masters degree in modern Irish history in August 2000, she moved to Italy for two years. Since her return to Ireland in 2002 she has been teaching.

# The IRA in Kerry 1916–1921

**Sinéad Joy**

The Collins Press

Published in 2005 by
The Collins Press
West Link Park
Doughcloyne
Wilton
Cork

© Sinéad Joy 2005

Sinéad Joy has asserted her moral right to be identified
as author of this work.

The material in this publication is protected by copyright law. Except as may be
permitted by law, no part of the material may be reproduced (including by
storage in a retrieval system) or transmitted in any form or by any means,
adapted, rented or lent without the written permission of the copyright owners.
Applications for permissions should be addressed to the publisher.

British Library Cataloguing in Publication Data

Joy, Sinéad
    The IRA in Kerry, 1916-1921
    1. Irish Republican Army 2. Guerrillas – Ireland – Kerry –
    History – 20th century 3. Ireland – History – 1910-1921
    4. Ireland – History – War of Independence, 1919-1921
    5. Kerry (Ireland) – History – 20th century
    I. Title
    941.9'6

ISBN 190346479X

*Typesetting:* The Collins Press

*Font:* AGaramond, 11 point

Printed in Ireland by Colour Books

*Cover:* Oldtown Design

*Cover image:* Group of rebels from the north Kerry area, *c.* 1920,
from a private collection

# Contents

*Preface* vi
Introduction 1
The Unsettling Sound of Freedom 11
Greater Shocks to Come 26
'A Rank and File of Bogtrotters and Cannibal Natives' 42
The Will of the People or the Desire of a Few? 62
'The IRA Mob' 78
Likeable Tans and Unlikely Rebels 94
War in Peace: A Battle of Wills 108
Conclusion: A Very Different Rebel? 122
*References* 129
*Bibliography* 161
*Index* 173

# Acknowledgements

This book was originally researched and written as the subject of an M. Phil thesis for University College Cork four years ago. My interest in the period goes back much further though, to my pre-Leaving Certificate days and the classes of Mr Shane O'Shea at the Intermediate School, Killorglin. An inspirational teacher, it was he who first introduced me to the Irish Revolution and captured my imagination with it. I have him to thank for my interest in Irish history and much of what I have achieved in the area since.

I owe the research and completion of the book itself to a number of people. In writing the original thesis I was fortunate to have Dr Andy Bielenberg as my supervisor. He helped me in my efforts to locate relevant sources, he checked each chapter and always improved what I had written. In County Kerry, I want to thank Dr Jim Brosnan, Dingle, for all his help in locating papers for me for the book; Martin Moore, Tralee, for allowing me to view his remarkable photograph collection from the period, for reading and correcting the document, and sharing his knowledge and opinions on the period; from Killorglin, I want to thank Michael Ahern, Bernard Cronin, Francis McGillicuddy and John Galvin for their books and shared information; and I am indebted to Liam Crowley, in particular, for providing me with invaluable sources from the period. Thanks also to Kathleen Sugrue, Cromane, for her honest opinion on the work. I want to thank Thomas Byrne, Killorglin, who proof read the original thesis; Bridget Sheehan, Paddy Landers and Ger Lynch, south Kerry, who made inquiries about the war and rebel activists in that part of the county; and also Leo O'Shea, who spoke to me on the period when I first undertook the project in 1997. To Padraig and Neilie O'Sullivan, Beaufort, I am very grateful for providing some excellent contacts and all their help. I also want to acknowledge the staff in Tralee County Library, Cahirciveen Heritage Centre, University College Cork Special Collections and the University College Dublin Archive. I owe a great deal also to Helen O'Carroll in the Kerry County Museum who shared and directed me to some invaluable sources. I want to acknowledge the Casey family, Tralee, for permitting to view and use Con Casey's memoirs.

Thanks are due also to Michael D. O'Shea, Cahirciveen, who loaned me his books and took time to detail aspects of the war in Kerry, and Edward Quirke, New Jersey. Both men have died since work on this book started. Mr Quirke, a leading rebel in the struggle in north Kerry, took time to write to me and document his own experiences of the war. I hope I have done those reflections justice.

In the re-drafting of the thesis into book form I need to thank especially Maria O'Donovan and Fintan Lane, both of whom edited this work. I know it was the stuff of nightmares.

Finally, thanks to my family and my mother and father, in particular, for their encouragement and continuing support. This book would not have been possible without them.

SINÉAD JOY
*January 2005*

# Acronyms

| | |
|---|---|
| CAI | Cork Archives Institute |
| CI | County Inspector |
| GHQ | General Headquarters |
| IG | Inspector General |
| HQ | Headquarters |
| I/O | Intelligence Officer |
| IRA | Irish Republican Army |
| IRB | Irish Republican Brotherhood |
| ITGWU | Irish Transport and General Workers Union |
| KCL | Kerry County Library |
| KCM | Kerry County Museum |
| MA | Military Archives |
| NA | National Archives |
| NLI | National Library of Ireland |
| O/C | Officer in Command |
| PROL | Public Records Office, London |
| RIC | Royal Irish Constabulary |
| UCC | University College Cork |
| UCD | University College Dublin |

'It's almost 80 years since the flying column days. The people of Ireland *today* should not forget the sacrifices made by the men and women of the 1920s. I have a list of most of the casualties of Kerry. A lot of them grew up with me and some sat beside me in school. (They) made Ireland what it is today.'

*Edward Quirke's letters to the author*
*22 December 1997; 24 February 1998*

# Introduction

Probably the most striking feature of the local historiography on the War of Independence in County Kerry is the idea of rebels honour-bound to the ideal of a Republic. Local parish publications invariably show images of children 'with ballads of freedom on their lips' and souvenir pictures of the 1916 leaders in their pockets.[1] There are 'memories of fierce fighting'[2] in most of the articles written on the period, while the odd survivor will tell you that the rebels of Kerry were to the very end 'dedicated men',[3] as well as 'the finest of lads' who made Ireland 'too difficult a place for the English forces'.[4]

Another feature of the literature is the impression of relative equality within the IRA; this is apparent, for example, when one reads the popular compendia *Kerry's Fighting Story* and *With the IRA in the Fight for Freedom*, both of which were published by the Kerryman Ltd in the 1940s and 1950s. Likewise, both of these works portray the county as a significant area of operations during the Tan War, and the 'rebels' profiled invariably feature as heroes, 'undefeated, (and) undeterred by terrorism'. Officers are all men of 'surprising coolness and wonderful resourcefulness', showing 'recklessness in the face of danger' and living only for the 'glory' of the Republic.[5] The civil population is seen to 'cheerfully' obey the edicts of the new Dáil institutions and invariably appear as 'steadfast' supporters of the rebels.[6]

This traditional view is scrutinised in this study. New analyses of any kind always draw a degree of cynicism, but it was still interesting to note just how inflexible interviewees could be when discussing interpretations other than those laden with talk of republican boy-soldiers and crushing defeats. It is commonplace to describe nationalism as an essential component of the 'Irish rebel' and this nationalism was clearly an important motivator during Kerry's War of Independence: 'There had to be resistance to the British government' was the view expressed by one south Kerry man interviewed, who justified this remark in terms of a nationalist re-awakening, caused by the 1867 Fenian uprising and the land wars of the 1880s.[7] 'Evictions and agrarian trouble heighten(ed) nationalist feelings in Kerry', agreed J.J. Barrett in *In the Name of the Game*. He wrote:

> It is reasonable to say that an innate resentment to the landed gentry was present in most Kerry people, or even most Irish people, in the decades leading up to the War of Independence.
>
> Memories of evictions, unreasonable taxes and run down estates due to absenteeism fuelled such resentment and distrust.[8]

Traditional accounts of the period often refer to the 'unflinching patriotism' of local communities. They were wholly committed to independence and loyal to the rebel cause. Can we be so certain,

*Introduction*

however, that the 'unflinching patriotism' so often found in traditional accounts was genuinely reflective of the attitudes of the county's population during the independence campaign? Did the Reverend M.D. Forrest give an accurate representation when he wrote in 1920 of ageing mothers with 'their heads bowed in sorrow over a murdered son, but whose hearts are throbbing with pride at the thought that their loved ones have died for Ireland'?[9] And what of the fighting men themselves? Is it fair to say that the rebels of Kerry were, as is the common assumption, a militarily efficient outfit and a conscious revolutionary force? Did they use their resources to maximum effect and wage 'a ceaseless fight against enemy occupying forces'?[10] Who were the people who joined the Kerry IRA and what were their motives? What was their general character and were they really the 'rowdy' lot[11] police officials declared them to be?

The aim of this study is to address these questions and to consider whether the traditional interpretations surrounding the war are fair assessments of what actually occurred in the county during the 1916-21 period. Attempts will also be made to measure the actual extent of IRA activity in the county, seek explanations for it, and place the significance of such activity on a wider, national scale through comparisons with other regional studies.

It has been well documented that the campaign meant radically different things to different people. Lady Albinia Broderick, sister of Lord Midleton, was sufficiently inspired by the nationalism of the day to change her name into the Gaelic, Gobnait Ní Bhruadair, and to give shelter to men on the run in her big house in Cahirdaniel. 'It was during the troubles in the mountains', recalled Bill Tangney, one of the many who experienced her almost fanatical fervour for the cause.

I was in the column out there, there was 25 of us altogether. She was helping us and looking after us and bringing us clothes and she had posters for this and for that to join the IRA – and she'd be up there at the head of the table telling everything.[12]

Lady Edith Gordon, likewise, while not as intense about her politics, was equally deliberate about showing her support. 'Ever since I had thought about the matter at all I had been a Home Ruler', she wrote in 1934, 'but I have never been able to take politics with the same seriousness with which my 'die-hard' neighbours took their unionism. That I should hold opinions so utterly at variance with theirs seemed to them a betrayal of my class'.[13] Demanding sedition and violent rebellion at every turn was not, it seems, in the Kerry case at any rate, all that necessary to being a good republican.

Neither would it seem that republican values and a sense of honour were essential attributes of the rebel soldier. In fact, recent historiography has found that military discipline among the IRA and their political motivation are profoundly suspect. 'Murder', according to Peter Hart, was more common among the rebels of Cork than battle. 'They were young, tough and barely under the control of their superiors', he argued in his 1998 study on the Cork IRA. He further claims that,

The revolution produced many skirmishes and casualties by combat, but many more people died without a gun in their hands, at their doors, in quarries or empty fields, shot in the back by masked men.[14]

That 'murder became commonplace' is also a view expressed by

*Introduction*

Michael Laffan, 'whether it was carried out by the crown forces, by the IRA, or as a result of private hatreds'. 'As always happens in such conflicts', he wrote, 'the vulnerable were exploited and private scores were settled in the name of principle or patriotism.'[15] Whether this was the case in Kerry will be teased out later as will the issue of rebel conduct and their behaviour towards those they perceived as the enemy.

One of the central questions surrounding Marie Coleman's study on the Irish Revolution in County Longford was what prompted seemingly ordinary people to suddenly turn revolutionary?[16] 'Considerable group pressure' has been cited by Joost Augusteijn as one of the main factors in determining the level of involvement by the Mayo and Tipperary Volunteers,[17] while Coleman herself rated the absence of parental opposition and the presence of a republican tradition as hugely significant.[18] Hart, on the other hand, felt that the consideration of all three was necessary to explain the motivation of many of the Cork fighters.[19] 'The majority of rebels seem to have regarded their political choices as completely natural and their motives self-evident', he wrote.

If you had the right connections, or were part of a certain family or circle of friends, you became a Volunteer along with the rest of your 'crowd'. If not you probably stayed outside or on the fringes; for the majority of Volunteers the decision to join was a collective rather than an individual one.[20]

Charles Townshend, Tom Garvin and David Fitzpatrick, meanwhile, have, at different times, each cited the quest for land as the underlying factor in explaining rebel activity during this period. 'Residual land hunger' was what Tom Garvin called it: 'Land had been offered to IRA men' and 'fear of losing this land is the main reason why the IRA wish(ed) to accept only an Irish Republic and nothing else,' he has insisted.[21] Likewise, David Fitzpatrick found that in County Clare IRA engagements were in many cases 'thinly disguised land seizures which Headquarters had neither the ability nor perhaps the intention to prevent.'[22] What will be considered during the course of this study is whether the land question was an equally contentious issue in Kerry and, if it was, was it this and not notions of a republic that fuelled the independence campaign?

It certainly seems that the rebels knew enough to appreciate that they were not going to get very far on the independence front without some guarantee of land redistribution. How central IRA General Headquarters (GHQ) was to the fight will be considered, as will the input from local IRA leaders on the ground.

David Fitzpatrick, for one, remains highly sceptical of any significant influence having being exerted by GHQ on local IRA command. His own research into the Clare IRA concluded that had GHQ been more forthcoming with weapons, it would have been in a better position to control the provincial campaign. According to Fitzpatrick:

> The more fugitive, isolated and self-dependent the columns became, the harder it was for any outsider to influence their conduct, however high his rank; at first glance one might suppose that the Volunteers were being steadily consolidated into a centralised and disciplined, if not very effective, national army. But in the moonlit world of flying columns, central authority and the national interest cut far more shadowy figures than the Mulcahy Papers would have us suppose.[23]

Charles Townshend also concurred with this view, stating that

*Introduction*

GHQ remained 'something of a make-believe high-command'.[24] 'Companies chose their own officers and never entirely accepted the hierarchical control implicit in the term "army"', he insisted. 'They remained first and foremost groups held together by personal or local loyalties.'[25]

Generally speaking, most historians have little difficulty in accepting that the control exercised by GHQ was for the most part theoretical, but there are those who would argue that the role of the central command has actually been understated. Coleman's work on Longford has shown that, even though there was little available from GHQ in the way of weaponry to the county (one of the main reasons cited by David Fitzpatrick for the failure of a central command), Seán MacEoin, one of the highest ranking officers in the region, would rarely attempt an ambush without first seeking headquarters approval.[26] 'The role of IRA General Headquarters in directing the military campaign has been reassessed and found to be much more significant than previously considered', she wrote. Coleman's study indicates that the general interpretations of the war are by no means properly reflective of what went on in the regions. By deviating in this way, she has shown an alternative to previously accepted claims and challenges other students of the period to test existing theories in relation to specific regional experiences. This book will examine where Kerry fits into this historiographical argument regarding the IRA and its relationship with GHQ.

The social composition of the county's rebels will also be discussed, and their composition will be compared with the findings of other historical studies. Charles Townshend has commented generally on the 'working-class complexion' of the IRA rank and file. 'In the provinces, farming backgrounds clearly pre-dominated, especially among officers', he attested. 'Outside the farming group, men from shops and trades tended to be replaced by labourers.'[27] Tom Garvin has also hinted at the high level of involvement by young men from the agricultural sector in the movement. 'Of IRA dead in 1919-21', he wrote, 'only one quarter had addresses in a large town or city, indicating that the force was far more than three-quarters rural. The younger sons of small and medium farmers, who had no alternative to emigration, appear to have been particularly active.'[28] Hart's analysis of the Cork Volunteers showed, nonetheless, that tradesmen and shop assistants provided the mainstay of support for the movement in the county, with farming families decidedly under-represented, providing only a quarter of the IRA's members outside the city.[29] Fitzpatrick, on the other hand, found that in Clare the sons of agricultural labourers were very strongly represented, particularly in the officer corps.[30]

From this it is again evident that standard interpretations of the war exist only as a predictor at best and can by no means be considered representative of the country as a whole. This study will aim to present Kerry's experience of the war, not so that it should fit neatly into any accepted theory, but so that it can draw its own conclusions and make its own mark, bringing us closer to a more complete understanding of what the struggle was all about.

On a final point, the claim that there was widespread acceptance of 'the Republic', and of the rebels who chose to 'defend' it, will also be subjected to some scrutiny. A number of contemporary historians, including Tom Garvin, have acknowledged that there was 'widespread acceptance' of the Dáil administration in many areas, 'partly for ideological reasons and partly because many people believed that the British were going to leave sooner or later; the

IRA, although sometimes merciless to those whom it regarded as collaborators, did not have to use terror as the vast bulk of the Catholic population accepted it as it had accepted various paramilitary local governments in previous generations', argues Garvin. He backs up this claim with the fact that Sinn Féin and IRA leaders, such as Collins, were able to walk around openly in the towns, be recognised by thousands of people, and not be reported to the authorities.[31] Others, like Peter Hart, have made the point that active resistance to the IRA was 'unusual', not because of any sense of loyalty to the republic, but because survival in revolutionary Ireland depended largely on submission.[32] The following chapters will focus on the extent of the actual support proffered by the civilian population, how sincere this support was, and the ways in which it was forced from the non-conformists. The methods employed by the IRA for silencing its opponents will also be examined within this context.

For students of the Irish Revolution the difficulty lies in separating fact from fiction, getting the real story instead of the official version. Popular thinking on the subject has remained relatively closed to new interpretations, but especially those that are not in keeping with the romanticised memory of the period. Traditional views of the campaign will nonetheless be scrutinised here in the light of available historical evidence. Primary source material, including letters and statements from the main players in the conflict, has been almost exclusively relied upon to give as accurate a picture as possible. Peter Hart's, David Fitzpatrick's and Joost Augusteijn's regional studies on the independence struggle have also proved invaluable, not only in providing me with a refreshing alternative to the sometimes gushing sentiment so often found in the earlier works on the period, but as a useful comparative guide for measuring Kerry against wider national patterns. Extensive use was also made of local histories and accounts of the war, including J.A. Gaughan's *Listowel and its Vicinity* and Jeremiah Murphy's *When Youth was Mine: A Memoir of Kerry, 1910-1921*, for furthering some of the general arguments. Implicit in any study like this is a sense of revisionism where the emphasis in interpretation shifts from the popularly accepted view. If anything, this study will aim not so much to rework conventional thinking on the period as to contribute to the history surrounding the guerrilla war in Kerry.

# 1

# THE UNSETTLING SOUND OF FREEDOM

> Like everything else in Ireland, my garden wore that summer an unsettled look. The political tension seemed to have obtruded itself into the herbaceous border where the bare stems of the slug-eaten phloxes wore an air of warning, of greater shocks to come.[1]
> *Lady Edith Gordon on Easter 1916*

THINKING BACK on his time as a resident magistrate in County Kerry, Lieutenant Colonel C.P. Crane found it hard to recall a dissenting Irishman. Kerry was 'perfectly quiet' at the time of his commission in 1901. 'The generation of moonlight disorder and crime had passed away almost entirely', he remembered.

> (A) new spirit was taking possession of the country; a spirit of harmony and understanding between class and class, giving hope that Ireland was at last going to fulfil her destiny and become a prosperous and law-abiding part of the Empire – a strength and not a weakness.[2]

Con Casey, a rebel and veteran of the independence movement, agreed with him. In his view a strong pro-British sentiment was definitely perceptible in the county: 'Looking back on that period,' he reminisced, 'I now realise how Anglicised we were.' 'The elders', excited by the pleasing prospect of Home Rule, 'had their eyes turned towards London', while, 'the young boys found pleasure reading periodicals and magazines intended for English boys. The doings, the adventures and the game loving of Harry Wharton, Bob Charry and others, as well as of the fat and food loving Billy Bunter had dulled for Irish boys the admiration they should have had for local and national heroes'.[3]

Liam MacGowen was one of those boys reared near the 'Big House' on the east side of Valentia Island. He too read the fashionable English journals, mentioning in particular, *The Sphere* and *London Illustrated News*. He even attended parties to celebrate King George's Coronation: 'We drank cocoa from cups decorated with that monarch and his wife Queen Mary. And we collected cigarette pictures displaying splendidly dressed generals like Kichener and Haig and Foch and the King of Romania.'[4]

There was something very high class about British culture. British gentlemen were distinguished, and British ladies fashionable. They were different to the Irish for all the right reasons. They had breeding, money, 'nice talk'[5] and the best land. To be seen as part of the British set guaranteed definite standing in a community. Tralee's postmaster, an Englishman, was one of that set; he was 'a personage of the highest rank' who 'came to work in top hat, black frock coat and striped trousers, exuding authority'.[6] On Valentia Island too, though the West Britons lived beside the 'Irish speakers with their funny names', there was a certain dress code, depending on which side of the divide you came from. The women on the east side wore fashionable costumes and toque hats; the women on the west wore black or yellow shawls. The men on the east side wore neat blue suits; those in the west wore long frieze coats, with double buttons above the split at the back.[7]

The gentry had their place in society and the local population was kept in theirs: 'Admittance beyond the gateway and the lodge was strictly controlled,' according to Casey. 'Very few were ever seen walking leisurely inside the walls, except pram-pushing mothers or nursemaids with passes that had to be purchased at the estate office in Denny Street,'[8] he recalled.

The gentry held position in society and the poorer locals were made aware of that. For years regard for those of exalted rank was upheld by the common man, and caused little resentment, on the surface at least. That situation was accepted until the Republicans started to mobilise. Class difference and dissatisfaction found a voice through the Republican movement, and often in a violent manner. MacGowen, in particular, described how the mood of the Irish-speaking westerners on Valentia Island changed suddenly in 1918 with 'more (of them) coming to our house and there were strange meetings and behind the house men shot at tin cans with .22 rifles.'[9] Lady Edith Gordon, living at Caragh Lake, felt the Irish were losing sight of the traditions of deference that was the due of her class. 'Among the old,' she wrote, 'a measure of respect and even friendship still obtained, but from the young, the slouching youth (who) props itself against the hedge and is to be seen spitting from the parapet of every bridge into the river below, instead of greeting, cap-touching – averted glances. Completely gone between them was any feeling of friendship, going, almost gone, every trace of the good manners for which the Irish peasant was once famed.'[10]

E. O'Gerity, the RIC county inspector, also picked up on the change in attitude. He believed that land-grabbing within Sinn Féin was the cause of the tension rather than class difference: 'The idea being to burn out all the old gentlemen's country houses to keep the old families from returning after "Peace" and to grab their demesne lands.'[11] For him, the land issue was the key to the changing mood. Ironically this was true for the Republicans also, but they did not see it in terms of O'Gerity's land grabbing. They were taking back land for the dispossessed Irish. The land they were claiming, they felt, was originally and rightfully theirs. There existed, nonetheless, particularly among the older generations, an inherent respect for the established order. Even Ernie O'Malley, the leading IRA figure, noticed it and was forced to drill country Volunteers in demesne land to rid them of what he called 'the ascendancy mind'. 'Even yet their fathers touched their hats to the gentry and the sergeant of the police,' he despaired.[12]

For the most part, land reform during the 1880s had transformed the outlook and social expectations of the Kerry community. While in 1880 farmers were still answering to the 'Big House', by 1900 farmers had control over their own plot of ground, and held all the confidence and sense of place that that brings. This was the reason Lady Gordon found the locals so changed. Irish society was in a state of flux and tenant farmers were taking a more active role in the social and administrative sectors of their communities. Literacy levels had improved in the county during this period; in 1911, 86.5 per cent of the population over nine years of age was able to read and write.[13] Economically, 'things were looking up'.[14] Rents had been appreciably reduced during this period by an estimated 40 per cent and successive land acts had enabled tenants to buy their own land.

A vast improvement was reported in rural living conditions, helped by the general recovery of farm prices in the 1890s. Cash incomes increased during this period, made evident by the gradual replacement of credit dealings with cash. Deposits in post office savings banks in a number of counties, including Kerry, rose from £250,000 in 1881 to almost £2,250,000 in 1912.[15] Shops and businesses in the larger towns increasingly widened their commercial appeal. Hillards of Killarney, for instance, was sending some 10,000 copies of its price index to the names on the electoral lists in Kerry within a radius of 30 miles of the shop.

The population of Kerry in 1911 amounted to 159,691 persons, 97.2 per cent of whom were Roman Catholic. The census indicated that the three main towns, Tralee, Listowel and Killarney, had a combined population of slightly over 19,000, showing that Kerry was, during this period, rural and Catholic, with agriculture supporting much of the local industry in the principal towns.[16]

The agricultural sector was by far the largest source of employment for men also, creating work for some 34,366 or 72.5 per cent of an overall male workforce of 47,427. Furthermore, of the 68,708 women classified as part of the 'indefinite and non-productive class' the majority were in fact members of farmers' families working on the land. Only 1,734, or 2.5 per cent, of women were actually classified as farmers or grazers, however, while a further 311 were employed on a farm either as agricultural labourers or as house servants. The census also shows that a significant number of the 4,913 persons categorised as general labourers were most likely employed as agricultural labourers.

TABLE 1. *Returns of 1911 Census for County Kerry*

| | |
|---|---|
| TOTAL POPULATION | 159,691 |
| Population aged 9 years and upwards | 127,672 |
| Roman Catholics | 155,220 |
| Literate | 110,469 |
| Killarney R.D. | 30,190 |
| Killarney U.D. | 5,792 |
| Listowel R.D. | 26,812 |
| Listowel U.D. | 3,409 |
| Tralee R.D. | 31,383 |
| Tralee U.D | 9,795 |
| Workforce (male) | 47,427 |
| Employed in Agriculture | 34,366 |
| General Labourers | 4,913 |
| Indefinite/non-productive | 68,708 |

From these figures, it can be generally estimated that in 1911 over 65 per cent of the population of the county was involved to some extent in agriculture. The census returns nevertheless revealed that of the 61 per cent officially employed within the agricultural sector, 26,635 (73 per cent) were part of farming families working their own land, while farm labourers were left distinctly on the margins, accounting for only 23 per cent of the agricultural workforce.[17] The fortunes of the agricultural labourer had been improving since the 1880s, with a gradual increase in wages and the introduction of various housing schemes. The farmers' boys of Kerry were, nevertheless, still forced to supplement their incomes as part-time poets, cobblers, tailors and barbers.[18] In 1918, wages were about double what they were 60 years previously,[19] yet this increase, described as 'considerable', had not advanced in proportion to the increased cost of living and it was, according to the police authorities, 'a matter of surprise that there (was) not more distress'.[20] Labourers found it increasingly 'impossible to make ends meet' as prices soared during the war years, a combination of profiteering and the great demand for food.[21]

The farming class, on the other hand, did well out of the war. Harvests were good and the continuing high prices helped line their pockets. The labourers' wages were inconsistent, however, and frequently varied from farm to farm.[22] It was the introduction of the 'out of work' donations towards the end of 1918 that best illustrates the inadequacy of the labourer's wage at this time: 'hundreds' of labourers left their employment in 1919 to avail of the higher sum offered by the government.[23]

Slighted in society, they were, according to John B. Keane, likened to 'low-down latchikoes that (had) to be kept in their proper place'.[24] Motivation to join the Volunteer movement came from a number of factors – patriotism, adventure and fear of conscription – and for the labourers it was the promise of land and the chance to better their position in the community. Michael Brennan, active with the Clare brigade, admitted in the early 1960s that IRA officers on the whole used land agitation as a cover in an effort to organise the Volunteers. 'I may as well tell you,' he confided, 'I hadn't the slightest interest in land agitation, but I had every interest in using it as a means to an end, the end being to get those fellows into the Volunteers and once they were in you could do something with them.'[25]

'There was a policy,' explained IRA veteran Dan Mulvihill, 'of taking over the land that had been taken from people evicted up to

80 years before. This was stopped, however, as it could have wrecked the country.'[26]

Headquarters also demanded a stop to all agrarian disturbances.[27] In Kerry land had always been, according to a 1921 police report, 'at the root' of all trouble.[28] It was made more difficult by having 'at its back not Sinn Féiners but simply blackguards'[29] in the words of one nationalist. The demand for land in the county only increased as the conflict escalated, often taking from republican aspirations and the struggle for a national ideal. 'I am making no secret of my belief that this will destroy the Republican movement here', wrote Dr Sheehan from Milltown, a medical officer with the Kerry No.1 Brigade.[30] Cattle-driving, illegal ploughing and the forceful seizure of plots had plunged many areas of the county 'into a state of anarchy'.[31]

The officers in the Kerry No. 2 Brigade had managed 'to get matters some way in hand' by June 1920,[32] but in the Kerry No. 1 Brigade area, where the number of agricultural labourers was proportionately higher than in the rest of the county, the agitation for land had become so serious that in some districts of north Kerry labourers had taken to fighting among themselves. 'In almost every case where farms have changed hands,' reported one county inspector, 'there is agitation amongst the labourers and smallholders to have the farms divided up amongst them and those who do not get a share are dissatisfied and have resorted to outrages on the plotholders.'[33] Colonel Hickey, who owned a substantial land holding in Ballybunion, had to move his family out of the county, believing it to be 'no longer safe to live in'.[34] Meanwhile, in Killorglin, a dispute over ownership rights to a watercourse culminated in one local farmer having his ears severed in January 1919.[35]

According to the police reports, republicanism meant little to

*The Unsettling Sound of Freedom*

the agricultural labourer whose motives in joining were generally founded 'in the hope of acquiring someone else's property'.[36] The labourers of ther county were not the only group of Kerry society out for themselves at this time though, if going on what these reports say. After the Redmondite split in 1914, Irish Volunteer companies reorganised under factions of nationalist dissidents. They attracted only a fraction of the initial Volunteer membership in the county. The huge support for Redmond during the early months of the war was largely a result of the success of his party's successes in the pre-war years. The Irish parliamentary party had worked hard for peasant proprietorship and although progress was slow between 1881 and 1907, it was, according to academic opinion, always steady enough to maintain the party's power base in rural areas.[37] In November 1914, for example, almost three months after the split, Kerry's Redmondite National Volunteers accounted for 81 per cent of an estimated Volunteer membership total of 5,575 men.[38]

The 'influentials', or 'those who had a stake in the county', were particularly voluble in their support for John Redmond during this period, while the priests were believed to be so tied to the old Irish party and its policies that Ernest Blythe 'had not the nerve to call on a priest in Cork or Kerry on the off-chance that he might be favourable to us'.[39] Admittedly, there were a number of younger curates who appeared a little 'hot-headed' (sympathetic to the republicans), but according to Hugh O'Hill, the RIC county inspector during this period, there were no more than four young priests officially associated with the movement. The majority of parish priests were hostile and in some cases actually succeeded in preventing the formation of Irish Volunteer branches.[40]

By the spring of 1915, however, public opinion was becoming

more alert to the realities of war on the Western Front. One contributor to the Tralee notes of the Workers' Republic provided some insight into the changing mood when he wrote,

> A Ladies Battalion of soldiers' dependants from historic Mary Street paraded the streets a few nights last week in fighting attitude, cheering for John Redmond (happy man!) and waving sundry union jacks and Royal standards. The usual quiet of the town once more prevails, thanks to the clergy and some Tralee boys who, when things were becoming unbearable, made preparations to give the disorderly paraders a hot reception in one particular part of town. If there is a recurrence of such disgraceful conduct the manhood of the town will only have to take matters into their own hands, and beat these unsexed females back to their dens.[41]

Support for Redmond's National Volunteers was falling and many members began transferring their loyalties to local Irish Volunteer companies. In March 1915, Mr E. O'Connor of the Tralee branch of the Irish Volunteers complained that too many local Redmondites were 'anxious' to enter their corps. The executive committee was forced as a result to consider measures which would prevent 'undesirables' from joining the ranks.[42]

The Tralee branch was undoubtedly the most adept Volunteer unit in the county at this time, complete with a full-time instructor, 120 rifles and 12 pikes.[43] Apart from the occasional show of force by Austin Stack and his fellow activists, however, general Volunteer activity in the county was only mildly disruptive and by no means seriously intimidating. A disgruntled Sir Morgan O'Connell, though loud in his condemnation of Volunteer sedition, was still of a mind to inform the Rebellion Commission in May 1916 that 'whenever one met these bodies on the roads they were well conducted and considerate for other traffic'.[44] Progress was slow in many areas and the development of a unit depended ultimately on the perseverance of local leaders and on the depth of their enthusiasm for the cause. The 'excellence' of an Irish Volunteer company in the Cahirciveen area before the Rising can be attributed to 'local effort',[45] and it was generally considered to be one of the strongest battalions in the county, with an armoury of 57 rifles and fifteen revolvers.[46]

Ernest Blythe discovered on his return to Kerry in 1915 that although a number of branches in west Kerry had lapsed over the winter, it proved relatively easy to revive old companies once the 'best local men' were urged to regroup. 'Seán Óg MacMurrough Kavanagh's group in Dunquin had held together,' wrote Blythe approvingly, 'and Padraig Ó Brian and others in Ballyferriter had maintained undiminished activity.'[47] The presence of Desmond Fitzgerald, an avid Irish Republican Brotherhood (IRB) sympathiser, who set up house in the area in 1913,[48] or the crowds of Gaelic enthusiasts who were known to throng the streets of Dingle town, all assisted in the organisation of the Volunteers and can arguably account for the efficiency of the west Kerry branches during the early years of the movement.[49] In the Killorglin area, however, Blythe's efforts to re-establish a company had met with cold indifference. Local Irish language teachers, while sympathetic to the cause, were unable to give the names of any young men worth his while contacting and Blythe had to act on the advice of an old Sinn Féiner who suggested that he 'get out of the town by the first train next morning as nothing could be done in Killorglin'. In Kenmare, Blythe continued, 'the situation was not much better' with the majority of young Volunteers refusing as yet to become publicly identified with the movement. In many areas, Volunteer membership had been affected by an aggressive Redmondite campaign; tacitly supported by the clergy and conservatives of the county, they were using threats of unemployment, eviction, and the denial of old-age pension benefits to undermine the membership of the Irish Volunteers.[50] In some areas it had the desired effect. Over half of an 80-strong company failed to appear for drill practice in north Kerry after rumours circulated locally that Volunteers could face eviction if they attended.[51] Progress in the Listowel area, likewise, was damaged by personal differences between members, while in Killarney, organisers met with resistance from a group who were adamant that they were 'neither for (Eoin) MacNeill nor (John) Redmond.'[52]

By the spring of 1916, however, almost two years after the split with Redmond, the Kerry Irish Volunteers had an estimated membership of roughly 1,093 persons. This accounted for just over fifteen per cent of the overall national membership.[53] Moreover, the Kerry branches possessed 397 rifles between them or 22 per cent of the 1,820 rifles held nationally.[54] Observers have interpreted the comparative success of the Irish Volunteer movement in the county as a straightforward reflection of the strength of nationalist feeling in Kerry. Ernest Blythe, however, writing almost 40 years later, was less certain of this: 'On the whole, conditions in Kerry were very much better than in Cork and the tide was flowing with us there.' But, he continued, there were times when 'I felt I was back in the North dealing with young IRB men who would do anything for Ireland but come out into the open.'[55]

They remained a minority, even though the National Volunteers were by that stage fading. In fact, the Irish Volunteers still had just 31 per cent of the combined Volunteer membership by April 1916.[56] Was the minority position the result of the aggressive Redmondite campaign pursued in the weeks immediately following the split? Or did it come from a general resolve among other Volunteer branches to follow the example set by the Tralee branch in 1915 to stop the 'undesirable' local Redmondites from rejoining their ranks? Either way, republican rhetoric was of little interest to the average man who was troubled by the more mundane issues of pensions, cattle prices and potato crops. 'That same freedom,' cried one Blasket Island fisherman, 'has me deafened and I don't even know what it means.' Liam MacGowen also insisted that 'there were many who were too wrapped up with the need to eke out a fishing and farming existence to bother about the new Fenianism'.[57]

The 'new Fenianism' had its advantages, however. The evidence shows that a good many joined the movement to avoid conscription. The agricultural basis of Kerry society meant that the sons of farmers or shopkeepers could have been denied parental permission to enlist, or perhaps they showed little inclination as a result of the sudden prosperity and the labour shortage on the land. The young men of the county may have found refuge in the anti-recruiting campaigns of the Irish Volunteers. An article entitled 'An Outsider's Impression of Kerry' carried in a number of the Kerry newspapers in June 1916 reckoned that the country people were indeed growing 'fat and prosperous' on the war with 'a great many joining the Sinn Féin movement and using it as a kind of umbrella for not fighting'.[58]

This argument is further strengthened by the Volunteer membership returns. The period of sharpest growth for the Kerry Volunteers was in late 1915 when the movement capitalised on the people's fear of conscription and on the recruiting letters that were being sent to young men of military age. Membership of the Irish Volunteer movement in the county increased by 20.3 per cent during this period, from 1,018 members in October 1915 to 1,278 members in February 1916.[59] This indicates that Volunteers' motives in joining came just as much from a fear of being conscripted to the British armed forces as enthusiasm for the nationalist cause.

Hugh O'Hill, RIC county inspector, candidly informed the Rebellion Commission in May 1916 that until John Redmond had declared in favour of recruiting 'the Sinn Féin movement was of no account'.[60] He warned, furthermore, that the strength of republican feeling in the county could hardly be ascertained from Volunteer numbers when many within its ranks 'thought they were insulted when they were called MacNeillites'.[61] Significantly, the participation by many of the more avowed republicans was seldom inspired by any highly developed sense of nationalism, but originated usually in local or familial traditions of resistance upheld by the ageing Fenian band.[62] 'If I had the misfortune to meet one of those old Fenians,' recalled Billy Mullins, 'he would have me jammed up against some shop door or window to drive his ideas home to me as to how useless it was for the Irish Party going over to England. They would tell us "There is only one cure for it, boy, and that's the gun, boy, the gun."'[63] The Volunteer movement certainly represented a convenient cover for IRB reorganisation, but for many more the Volunteers continued as little more than 'a roll call'. This did not make the IRB set less radical, however, and as early as 1914 IRB organisers sent in to review the Kerry Volunteers forcefully intimated the need for a 'blood sacrifice' and invited likely agitators to prepare for armed insurrection. Austin Stack, according to one Tralee officer, 'impressed on (the men) the desirability of going to Confession and being prepared spiritually to die at any time'.[64]

The prospect of an armed insurrection strengthened the patriotic resolve of many young nationalists, and certainly there were those who regarded their participation almost as a sacred calling. May Dálaigh recalled how she watched her brother Tom cry bitter tears as he watched their father leave without him at Easter 1916: 'It took Charlie with all his persuasion to stop him going.' She remembered that, 'He sat there in that chair and he put his head down between his hands and he said we deprived him of the one thing in his life that he looked forward to.'[65] But where self-sacrifice and loyalty to the Republic featured as Daly's motives, 'fun', 'the sense of adventure', and having 'an alternative to football and hurling' are strongest in other veteran accounts.[66] These were the boys, 'divested of trenchcoats and revolvers', who dressed up 'as usual' for the Wren on St Stephen's Day 'adorned with sashes and streamers of coloured ribbon'.[67] They were 'the belligerent youth'[68] of Lady Gordon's neighbourhood who regarded train raiding as a 'popular pastime' and drill practice as entertainment 'accompanied by much yelling and the beating of tin cans'.[69] They were only boys like Dan Mulvihill looking for where next they could get their 'kicks'.[70]

So where did the Republic come into it all? It didn't. Not in 1915 when land issues and the threat of conscription had the ordinary man troubled. These troubles were the making of the IRA in Kerry, however, and provided the base from which the independence fighters were eventually drawn.

# 2

# Greater Shocks to Come

The 'great madness' of Easter 1916 affected only a small number of people in Kerry.[1] Three hundred Volunteers from around the county mobilised in Tralee on that Easter Sunday morning, and big turnouts were also reported for Listowel and Castlegregory.[2] However, beyond that little happened. Most areas in the county continued as either 'quiet' or 'normal'. The increase in police activity during this period, along with the arrests of the more prominent leaders in the movement, contributed to a 25 per cent decline in membership in the four months after the rebellion.[3] Public reaction to the failed rebellion was also a factor in undermining support. 'Mothers and fathers urged their sons not to have anything to do with a movement which looked more dangerous than it had heretofore appeared,' wrote Blythe,[4] and the RIC, according to Ed Quirke 'needed only the slightest provocation to make an arrest'.[5] Volunteering had suddenly become dangerous and this impacted hugely on an organisation which up to that point was seen by a lot of the men involved as something 'new and a lot of fun for a while.'[6]

*Greater Shocks to Come*

The reaction of the people to the executions in Dublin was also level headed enough. Mournful faces were reported in Killorglin, but, according to the *Kerryman*, this had more to do with 'the fact that there was not a drop of Guinness to be had in the town'.[7] The working classes of the county, meanwhile, were more worried about the damaged potato crop and 'the prospect of dearer and scarcer food',[8] while in Tralee town, most locals were indifferent to the happenings in Dublin. It was all too good to be true for the RIC county inspector, Hugh O'Hill, who was delighted to report in June 1916 that, with the exception of Killarney and an area around Farranfore, the wave of sympathy for the executed Sinn Féin leaders was on the decrease in county places.[9] By the autumn of 1916, however, the mood of the people was changing. The hanging of Roger Casement in August was keenly felt in Kerry and the police were for the first time encountering 'a quiet spirit of disloyalty'.[10] 'The whole country seems to be crying,' wrote the republican Thomas Ashe to his sister Minnie. Even the most unlikely sympathisers were affected.[11] Henry Brassil, an Englishman based in the county, thundered at the decision to hang Casement. 'The sentence is a terrible one,' he exclaimed. 'To put it mildly it is atrocious and barbarous.'[12] Likewise, Lady Edith Gordon and her unionist neighbours were 'horror struck' at the severity of sentences imposed. They even refused to sow sweet pea that year as a protest against the policy of the government 'every member of whom (they) would like to see hanging from a lamp-post.'[13]

Public outrage also saw an increase in the number of petty assaults against the RIC and known British sympathisers. Groups of Volunteers, overlooked by the police authorities after the failed rebellion, now defiantly congregated 'in clubs or halls and at street-corners'.[14] Police held them accountable for the general state of unrest, perhaps unjustifiably. Disorganised and effectively leaderless, this 'rowdy' Sinn Féin element lacked direction and appealed to only a fraction of the population. Consequently, by late autumn senior RIC officials were satisfied that public goodwill in the county had begun to improve. The level of policing in turn lessened considerably. It was relaxed to such an extent that the local RIC in many areas went back to the old way of doing things, which included the odd breach of a regulation. 'I cannot understand it,' lamented F.P.S. Taylor, a Dublin Castle official, on reading that a District Inspector in the county granted 60 gallons of petrol, or almost eight times the amount allowed, to a businessman in September 1916. This indiscretion prompted all kinds of wild speculation, including the assumption that Sinn Féiners were planning to store the petrol for use in an enemy submarine base.[15]

RIC violations were common enough in communities as insular as rural Kerry was during this period, a feature of life that may indicate that the constabulary in the county was not as hostile as popularly believed. 'They were prepared to dismount and chat up civilians,' wrote Con Casey, 'and when the time came for taking annual returns of livestock and crops they had access to every farmhouse in their charge and became acquainted with the occupants.'[16] Colonel Crane, who spent almost twenty years in the county as a resident magistrate, was often surprised by the 'neighbourly' regard of the local police in their treatment of noted offenders. 'I have often had a case,' he marvelled, 'where the RIC would ask for a chance to be given to a notorious disturber of the peace.'[17] 'The police at that time were very affectionate,' insisted another, while one ex-constable named Dunne, who was stationed in Kenmare, commented on 'a good friendly air' in the county where the police and the people 'all got on fairly well'.[18] 'On patrols you went along the road and had a chat with a farmer if you met a farmer,' he stated. 'We carried no arms at that time. We used to go out at night time and go along the road and, in fact, we'd go to a certain house and have a game of cards.'[19] The provincial nature of Kerry society can in part explain the good relationship that existed between the police and their communities. The fact that many rank-and-file RIC came from 'good farming stock', also strengthened that attachment. There was an extraordinarily high rate of enlistment in the RIC from the county, particularly among the younger farmers' sons whose only other option was emigration or an apprenticeship in one of the bigger towns.[20] In Kerry, as a result, 'you could hardly go into a house without a son in the police, or if they hadn't, they had a brother'.[21]

These apparent good relations between the police and the public were damaged during the final months of 1917 as the Sinn Féiners started to reorganise. 'In most parts of the county,' complained one RIC inspector in November 1917, 'the Sinn Féiners are sullen and unfriendly and in many places even the well-disposed are afraid to be noticed talking to a policeman.'[22] Dunne, the ex-RIC man, recalled how one young girl who came to the Kenmare barrack to report a murder dared not go inside but 'rushed away' again;[23] the inhabitants of Brosna, who in 1916 could not complain enough about the rebels 'for ruining the country', refused to inform on any of the Sinn Féiners who had pulled up all the potato stalks belonging to the police in the village and in neighbouring Ranalough and Scartaglin.[24]

Initially, it seems that the police were not hugely concerned by the change in attitude. Rather, they seemed to believe that the increased public support for Sinn Féin derived more from fear than from any real commitment to republican ideals. 'I do not believe,' announced County Inspector Heard, 'that the movement is taken as seriously by the bulk of the people as it was a short time ago, yet few could dare to say anything against it.'[25] Indeed, the evidence shows that there were many in the county who were decidedly opposed to republican methods during this period and were made uneasy by hostility towards the RIC. 'The people got on very well with the police until Sinn Féin started to organise,' stated Densie Collins of Ballydonoghue. 'That threw a spanner in the works and we were not allowed to go and mix with them after that. That was a bad situation!'[26] On Valentia Island, meanwhile, 'the formerly friendly policemen took to raiding houses and for the first time, Sergeant Coughlan, a decent man, awkwardly carried a black revolver.'[27]

Nevertheless, interest in the republican movement soared in the wake of the 1916 rebellion. The figures show a 478 per cent increase in the nominal membership during 1917 from 891 members in December 1916 to 5,149 by December 1917. This figure was practically doubled again during 1918 to 9,483 members.[28] The seemingly endless acclamation of the Easter martyrs, commemorated in speeches, requiem masses and a range of rebel memorabilia, invoked a sympathetic following even in the most isolated reaches of Kerry. This included the Great Blasket Island, where the pictures of Thomas Ashe (who on 25 September 1917 died as a result of forcible feeding while on hunger strike) and the 1916 leaders on Peig Sayers' wall 'were so secure that Oscar,[29] the strongest day he ever was, couldn't pull them down'.[30] The violent death of Ashe, in particular, appalled the wider community and was, without doubt, a huge factor in increasing support for the republican movement. Over 700

Volunteers from the county travelled to Dublin for the removal, while at home mock funerals were enacted in almost every parish.[31] The number of Volunteer clubs in the county, disregarded previously by the police authorities, 'came in then with a swing' acquiring almost 3,000 members in a matter of months.[32] Aside from this, and the fact that the Irish Volunteers had managed to retain its hardened core of support after 1916, the emergence of political Sinn Féin, controlled by older and more constitutionally minded nationalists, increasingly appealed to a wider electorate by offering a lively, yet safe, alternative to old party politics.

Heartened by the prospect 'of a more ample measure of Home Rule', the disillusioned supporters of the moderate patriotic organisations in the county, including the Irish Parliamentary Party and the more marginal United Ireland League, and Board of Erin, were now declaring themselves in favour of Sinn Féin.[33] Politically, in the words of the *Killarney Echo* in late 1918, 'Sinn Féin (was) a new thing, a movement without a past, an untried movement'.[34] In fact, the more republican members of the original Sinn Féiners were concerned at times about the sincerity of the new members whom they increasingly regarded as 'cloaked parliamentarians'. Indeed, some feared that political conservatism would take from the traditional physical-force principles that they were attempting to uphold.[35] This 'pack of idiots', according to one active republican in the county, was, after all, 'responsible for the discontent and ill-will which led to the Dublin outbreak.'[36] Talk in the Kerry newspapers of Sinn Féin's 'hand in glove' relationship with parliamentarism, and of crafty 'parliamentarians dressed in Sinn Féin clothing',[37] engendered fears that Irish Volunteer companies were in danger of playing second fiddle to the more political Sinn Féin.[38] Ultimately, however, the die-hards had little to worry about; political adventurers were few in number and, more importantly, it is clear that only a fraction of the politically conservative in the county were enthusiastic enough about radical republican values to seriously contemplate membership of the movement.[39]

Nationalist feeling in the county nonetheless increased after 1916. How widespread and significant was this surge of nationalist enthusiasm, and what brought it about? In terms of the economy, the Kerry community was enjoying unprecedented good fortune during this period and appeared relatively content with its lot. The executions of the 1916 leaders and the violent death of Ashe prompted the main increase in support for radical Sinn Féin. An examination of the membership figures shows that dread of the State's compulsory conscription into the army was also a factor for the increase. Indeed, the rate of affiliation to the republican movement was highest between October 1917 and November 1918 when the threat of conscription loomed largest (see Table 2). Nominal membership figures increased by over 900 per cent during this period, from 975 to 9,483 members. Sinn Féin and the Irish Volunteers practically tripled their membership, while the number involved with the republican Cumann na mBan (the 'league of women') was also seen to increase dramatically.[40]

Con Brosnan of Newtownsandes, an activist with the IRA's north Kerry flying column, attributed the increase in the fighting strength of his company to the 'conscription scare'. Membership of his unit increased from 20 to 150 men.[41] 'The constant advocacy of Conscription,' declared the RIC county inspector in March 1918, 'is keeping Sinn Féin alive more than anything else.'[42] It is worth noting that with the ending of the First World War in November 1918, this growth in membership virtually ceased. There was little

TABLE 2: *Sinn Féin and Irish Volunteer membership returns, July 1917-October. 1919*
(PROL, CO 904/103-110, RIC County Inspector monthly reports)

|  | *Sinn Féin:* | *Irish Volunteers:* |
| --- | --- | --- |
| July 1917 |  | 975 |
| November 1917 | 3,270 | 1,242 |
| February 1918 | 6,591 | 1,763 |
| May 1918 | 6,642 | 2,898 |
| September 1918 | 6,555 | 2,698 |
| January 1919 | 6,479 | 2,964 |
| May 1919 | 6,530 | 2,963 |
| October 1919 | 6,531 | 2,963 |

or no change in the nominal membership figures of the movement during 1919, while only an estimated 400 persons were believed to have joined either Sinn Féin or the Irish Volunteers during 1920.[43]

According to the RIC reports, the membership of Cumann na mBan also fell by almost 56 per cent in June 1919 from 327 members to 157. Membership figures, however, did recover during the spring of 1920 and exceeded the original membership total. The association acquired an additional 24 new members between April 1920 and June 1921.[44] This increase, in all likelihood, was considerably higher since the RIC relied on only limited information from the county.

It has been accepted generally that women republicans were often marginalised as the conflict progressed.[45] The majority of women who joined Cumann na mBan, moreover, came from nationalist backgrounds, with brothers or relatives already active

TABLE 3. *Membership Returns of Cumann na mBan,*
*January 1918-June 1921*
(PROL, CO 904/105-115, RIC County Inspector monthly reports)

| *January 1918* | *June 1918* | *January 1919* | *June 1919* |
|---|---|---|---|
| 124 | 327 | 327 | 157 |

| *January 1920* | *July 1920* | *January-June 1921* |
|---|---|---|
| 351 | 351 | 351 |

in the Volunteers, and it was not a case of just any woman joining. Cumann na mBan was very much a closed shop operation in Kerry. Any decline in membership figures was not out of fear of enemy reprisals or general disillusionment with the republican cause. Certainly, the stepping up of police activity against the clubs at this time does not seem to have diminished support. Rather, it was due more to the inactivity of the Volunteers during 1919, which rendered the supporting role of Cumann na mBan redundant. The resurgence in the organisation's membership during the summer of 1920 must, by the same token, have been due in large part to the return of previous members as Cumann na mBan activity increased when the conflict escalated.

The resolve of the Sinn Féiners as they prepared to resist conscription 'to the last man' attracted such widespread support at any rate that by June 1918 'practically all the farmers, their sons, labourers and shop assistants' were believed to have some affiliation with the movement.[46] Raids and night drilling became commonplace as rank-and-file Volunteers were advised to arm themselves properly for confrontation.[47] Government warnings were issued that tougher measures would be used to force through a Conscription Bill. 'If the Irish do not comply and continues with its policy For Ourselves Alone,' threatened one, 'Ireland will face economic isolation. By closing its ports against Irish produce, by denying to the island the advantages of imperial capital and credit, Great Britain could deprive the industries of the independent Republic of its only accessible market.'[48] An uneasy Austin Stack, writing from Belfast Jail in May 1918, was so convinced by the threats that he advised every household in the county to lay in supplies 'for the rainy day which threatens'. He suggested also that some of the money collected for the Defence Fund be invested in food stuffs such as flour and oatmeal. 'There is no better food than oatmeal,' declared Stack, 'and if the Kerry committees bought a couple of thousand pounds worth of this, it would be a prudent act.'[49] The county, meanwhile, was 'in hysterics'[50] at the thought of conscription. Demonstrations, strike action and rosaries for spiritual intercession were all employed in an effort to get the bill retracted. Lady Edith Gordon returned from London to find her local community in uproar: 'We had no trains, no posts, nothing but the wildest rumours. Conscription, it was said, was to be carried out by force. Everybody was to be taken, even the old aged.'[51] The police complained of men who still refused to enlist on the grounds that it was 'against their religion', while others were committing crimes in the hope of conviction and a lengthy jail sentence so as to avoid conscription to the army.[52]

The hysteria, however, clearly was not strong enough to loosen the purse strings of the county with regard to contributions to the Defence Fund. 'Kerry is not acting generally on any fixed basis in this matter,' mourned one correspondent for the *Killarney Echo*. 'In a small parish like Kilcummin, the first installment is £220 while

Kenmare sends only £200 – the same anomalies are everywhere!'[53] Inefficient collectors explains some of this: 'The collections are not concluded as quickly as is necessary in some parishes', complained one newspaper report in June, while later that month, collections 'in outstanding parts' were yet to be collected in several parishes in east Kerry.[54] In some areas, also, the disreputable character of Sinn Féin collectors dissuaded many from contributing to the fund. Accusations of Sinn Féin 'impostors pocketing funds' were rife in the north Kerry area.[55] There was some basis for these suspicions and in the little fishing village of Cromane, located five miles to the west of Killorglin and generally considered at this time to be one of the poorest areas in the district, the appointed collectors absconded with almost £100 worth of Sinn Féin funds.[56]

Sinn Féin was gaining notoriety and for all the wrong reasons. G.M. Heard, the RIC County Inspector, reported in February 1918 that 'persons who had been Loyalists and Unionists all their lives have owing to the fear of outrage and intimidation to pretend that they have leanings towards Sinn Féin'.[57] District Inspector Maunsell, meanwhile, who was working with the RIC Intelligence Branch in the Southern District, was appalled to learn that businessmen and merchants dependent on the favour of the public were subscribing to the Anti-Conscription Fund in an effort to deflect the antipathy of the Sinn Féiners.[58] Throughout the summer of 1918 businessmen in the county, who refused to sign an anti-conscription pledge, were frequently forced into submission by a general boycott insisted upon by local Sinn Féin clubs. 'So complete (was) the Sinn Féin system of terror,' despaired Heard, 'that no witnesses (could) be got to assist the police.'[59]

This shift in tactics among Sinn Féiners contrasts sharply with the more civilised behaviour of the earlier Volunteers. One possible explanation could be a strengthening in resolve of the no-compromise republicans after the Rising, or indeed it could have been the zeal of a more reckless element recently attracted into the movement. The conscription issue, and land agitation to a lesser extent, helped reposition the Sinn Féiners as 'defenders of the people' and boosted membership figures. These issues also introduced a 'bad type' to the movement who had little or no interest in republicanism or its ideals. Many were involved merely in pursuit of personal gain. The police authorities complained throughout the spring of 1918 that some Sinn Féiners were making full use of intimidation tactics to prosecute petty jealousies. In Caragh Lake the Volunteers were described as having 'sunk to the depths of infamy', when during the course of a raid, the gentry were robbed of some of their more valuable possessions.[60] 'Numbers of young men', grumbled Colonel Crane, 'who ought to have been in the army doing service for their country loafed about the corners of the streets, grasping at every straw as an excuse for not doing their duty.'[61] Sinn Féin's vigorous anti-conscription campaign provided a convenient cover for many to dodge military service. Others saw it as a fast track to getting land. Not all put much effort into their new political creed and during the 1919-21 period IRA battalion leaders were relying on the same men all the time to carry out the work. Con Brosnan assured an interviewer that almost all new members remained with his company after the scare and later proved to be 'very good and loyal Volunteers', but there still appeared to be only four or five men within each company whom local captains considered anyway 'reliable'.[62]

Both the business and farming sectors were particularly noted for their suspicions of Sinn Féin at this time. Calls for increased land redistribution and reduced food costs by prominent Sinn Féiners in the county alienated the more influential and affluent sections of the community. The number of labourers associated with the Sinn Féin movement, particularly in the north Kerry area, dramatically increased during this period with talk of better land and improved wages pulling them in. Weekly drill meetings in the Listowel district usually attracted about 40 or 50 men, yet this number could increase to over 1,400 Volunteers when land seizure was anticipated.[63] In fact, as a result of increased attacks on land and livestock, tension between the farmer and labourer was such that as early as 1918 police were reporting 'a split in the Sinn Féin camp' between the two factions. 'The farmers are realising,' noted County Inspector Heard, 'that the labourers are through the Sinn Féin movement getting too strong and are likely to get the upper hand.'[64] Farmers were eventually forced to form vigilance committees in an effort to protect their holdings[65] and although the movement attempted to detach itself from agrarian issues, outrages were still conducted in the name of Sinn Féin and the organisation continued to be held accountable for the disturbances.

Certainly, the 'farmers and shopboys', 'seriously frightened' by the conscription threat,[66] contributed generously to various Dáil Éireann subscription funds during this period, but both sectors continued as reluctant Republicans and only grudgingly, if ever, proffered their support for the movement. 'I object to my son being a Volunteer,' cried Patrick O'Shea, a prominent Killorglin businessman, on discovering that his son had defied his wishes and joined. 'I have a stake in the county and so has my son. There is no foundation to Sinn Féin, it is all rubbish. I live by the British Government and will not go back on it,' he continued.[67] The sentiments of the farming community were remarkably similar and attempts to damage Sinn Féin through the fictitious German Plot in May 1918 were met with widespread approval from this sector. County Inspector Heard reckoned that although the county in general did not accept the government claim of a German Plot, 'the average farmer (believed) otherwise and the great majority (were) relieved that their sons (were) for a time at least to be kept out of the ridiculous Republican movement'.[68]

Despite such fervent opposition to the movement from the farming class, police reports throughout 1920 continuously alluded to the overwhelmingly agricultural background of the Kerry IRA. 'The Volunteers,' declared one distraught county inspector, 'are ploughing by day and raiding by night', while another despaired that 'farmers (had) practically taken the lead in Sinn Féinism'.[69] An examination of the backgrounds of 70 Volunteers within the Rathmore company in east Kerry showed that 56 per cent of the group were farmers, or the sons of farmers, with a further nineteen per cent categorised as agricultural labourers. If one takes into account Con Casey's assertion that Volunteers with a skill or trade invariably came from a farming background, then it is possible that the number of Volunteers drawn from the agricultural class could amount to as high as 83 per cent altogether.[70] The relatively high proportion of people from farming backgrounds within the movement could be explained by the predominance of the agricultural sector within the county where 'the average man was either a farmer or labourer'.[71] This would not necessarily reflect a change in outlook, however, among the older farmers who were opposed to republicanism and its motives. While it is possible that there was a softening in attitude, or that opposition to the movement was not as hostile as previously outlined, it is more probable that the older farmers, who appeared desperate to keep their sons out of the 'ridiculous republican movement', eventually failed to contain their wilful offspring. Indeed, Jeremiah Murphy claimed that his involvement with a Volunteer company near his home in Killarney 'led to such bad feelings between father and son' that he 'decided to run away to some other part of the county'.

> Drilling and organising were carried out by night and farm work had to be done by day. Most of our parents didn't know where we spent our spare time and couldn't understand why we were so tired all the time.[72]

The atmosphere was so 'poisoned with suspicion', agreed Lady Gordon, that 'nobody dared express an opinion in public for as one old man whispered to me in confidence, "Your own son might be in it and you not know".'[73] These perspectives are significant in that they seem to confirm for Kerry that the republican movement that emerged after 1916 was essentially a young man's movement, fuelled as much by a reaction against convention as against British rule.[74]

Therefore, it is important to understand that many of the young Volunteers did not set out consciously to become part of an insurgency; rather, volunteering provided the repressed youth with the means to escape from what Peter Hart has called 'the traditional and predictable lines mapped out for him'.[75] 'It provided a brief escape from the tedium and frustration' was the view of one Cork Volunteer,[76] yet for Jeremiah Murphy, who watched his parents' world 'end at the horizon',[77] volunteering represented the means to cheat social or familial expectations and dared him to hope for something more out of life. 'These are the days of the young man,' heralded one Kerry newspaper, 'and instead of telling tales of *seanóreacht* we ought to deal with the young.'[78] Throughout the county there was a sense of change. How else could the older people though, 'weary with their interference' from the young, according to one County Inspector, 'not (be) allowed to have any minds of their own?'[79] 'Our time has come,' stated the young Charlie Daly to his brother at Easter 1916,[80] and though it was the conscription issue rather than any lofty nationalist aspiration that provoked the change in attitude from relative contentment with British rule to profound anti-British sentiment, it spurred a few republican young guns to act upon it and use the resentment to their own advantage.

# 3

# 'A RANK AND FILE OF BOGTROTTERS AND CANNIBAL NATIVES'

The English call them hooligans. They are the young idlers about the street corners who prefer mischief to work and flourish in times of disorder. They caught the fever if not the spirit of the Sinn Féin movement. Individualistic sniping, guerrilla warfare without the restraint of regular routine or discipline was all to the corner boy's taste.[1]

THE YOUNG fighters of the IRA could not have claimed to be a part of the so-called 'upper crust' of Kerry society. Neither were they what the British referred to as the 'peasant' Volunteers drawn from 'the black Irish of the bogs' or 'the mountainy men of the south and west'. C.H. Bretherton, special correspondent in Ireland for the *Morning Post*, typified a conventional view held among the British elite with his description of the Volunteers as a low breed 'spawned of the hewers of wood and drawers of water',[2] or a 'horde of proletarians, grocers, curates, farm labourers, porters, stable boys, car conductors and what not'; a collection of 'scum' and 'cornerboys'.[3]

'Fanatical youths and hired assassins,' was General Nevil Macready's view on them,[4] many of whom had little stake in the country.[5] Closer to home, RIC chiefs in the county felt they were dealing with 'rowdies' and a movement of 'young upstarts'.[6] The British officers in Killarney, 'some of them decent, some with swelled heads', generally regarded the IRA as 'savages'. For Volunteers, with the majority of them coming from homes that prided themselves on background and respectability, they could only laugh at such a view of themselves. 'I was the link between our fellows and the British forces,' wrote Dan Mulvihill who was appointed IRA liaison officer in the area shortly after the Truce, 'and knowing them and how they looked on us, it was good fun!'[7] The Volunteers who had to leave Killorglin town to go on the run were, likewise, considered 'all corner boys and a good riddance' by local businessman Patrick O'Shea.[8] In Killarney the Volunteer rank and file was, in the opinion of one local magistrate, composed of 'long haired pale faced youths'.[9]

The stereotype was well documented by the RIC and featured often in the police files of the time. Indeed, the type was so talked about in military circles that intelligence officers had to remind their colleagues that it was a mistake 'to imagine that rebels could be recognised through their uncouth state or peculiarities of 10'It (was) very difficult to distinguish between the offending and unoffending inhabitants,' agreed General Macready,[11] as 'armed men' were 'indistinguishable from peaceable civilians until they opened fire'.[12] Obviously the Volunteers the British forces encountered were at least respectable looking. The British assumption that they were of a low type was largely undeserved.

In fact, most Volunteer companies in the county had a reputation for hounding undesirables out of their communities. Rebels saw them as potential spy material for the British. Tinkers, tramps and drunken types[13] were not tolerated and the men that set out to remove them were, by and large, a class-conscious group who prided themselves on a decent upbringing. The *Tralee Liberator* was one of a number of newspapers that carried a front-page story in June 1920 telling of how the local Volunteers 'hunted those nomads of civilisation: those quarrelling and foul-mouthed visitors', the tinkers, out of Killarney town 'with a warning that should there be a repetition of their disgraceful conduct they would be severely dealt with'. 'It is not easy to frighten a tinker,' read the report, 'especially when he is surrounded by his pals who usually carry with them soldering irons, deadly weapons in the hands of infuriated men, but the Volunteers quietened them in a short time!'[14]

Lady Edith Gordon, who lived, like so many of her class, in fear of 'the wild men' roaming the Kerry countryside, was pleasantly surprised to find that the local Volunteers who arrived to raid her house one night were 'extremely tame'. 'The officer,' she marvelled, 'was polite and courteous,' and as 'the party clattered hastily past the stairs, back into the hall and out by the front door (they) apologised profusely as they went for having disturbed us!' 'They were', she added, 'very young and it was not unnatural to conclude that they were also very shy.'[15] Did Lady Gordon encounter the genuine article, a more civilised and respectable type of Volunteer? Or did she meet with the exception? These men were certainly not 'the low pack of robbers'[16] who had raided her neighbours the previous month. That experience testified to the existence of other unreliable IRA types abroad in the county at this time. The Irish Volunteers of Kerry

## 'A Rank and File of Bogtrotters and Cannibal Natives'

were a mix, morally speaking, and there were those who did not act out of respect for Republican principles.

It was not long before the more serious rebels of the county started to make a name for themselves, however. The motivation for these fighting men was clear cut. They had the single aim to drive all British influence from the island: 'Rebel commandos', 'terrorists' and reckless 'desperadoes' were some of the accolades given them by the RIC.[17] For the police the situation was rapidly getting out of hand. Republicans sensed it and veterans remember their supremacy in the fight with the British during those early months of the struggle. They 'flabbergasted the British' with their intelligence and military strategy. They valued a brand of Volunteer who was 'a bit wild'; such men within the movement were essential in order to give it the appearance of rebels hell bent on their goals.[18]

The suggestion that the Volunteer movement was made up of unskilled louts, unemployed, and of little social standing was, not surprisingly, categorically refuted by these active republicans. They equally resented any implication that their character was in any way disreputable. Con Casey remembered the Volunteers only as 'the laughing boys of the county! A gay, happy band of young men in good physical shape and enthusiastic about what they were engaged in.'[19] They were 'humorous', and described as 'bright and enterprising' by Lady Edith Gordon.[20] 'They were honest, fearless lads', according to Brian O'Grady, 'a credit to the parish they came from.'[21] Florence O'Donoghue, the Cork-based IRA officer and later historian of the movement, spoke of 'modest heroes shyly telling of their exploits' and of 'straight-limbed country boy(s)' dressed 'in (their) working clothes' who 'clicked their heels smartly and saluted as we went past. Being Kerrymen, they were proud to make a fuss over me. But I have reason to be proud of them.'[22] 'It would be hard to meet a better bunch,' wrote Dan Mulvihill of his fellow officers on the Kerry No. 1 Brigade Staff.[23] 'They were,' according to Con Casey, 'heavily on the side of abstinence' and, in John Joe Rice's experience, good Catholics being 'particular about duties and going to receive.'[24] Local newspaper reports meanwhile described the majority of young Volunteers who came before the county's magistrates for illegal drilling and other seditious offences as 'well-conducted', 'most respectable' and 'law-abiding young men'.[25]

William Huggard, a land agent kidnapped by IRA men near Castleisland in July 1920,[26] paid tribute to his captors speaking 'in terms of the highest praise of the courtesy, gentlemanly bearing and hospitality of those who kidnapped him and his caretaker Cooney'. 'Mr Huggard states,' went the report, 'that none of his captors wore any sort of disguise, but were of a fine, gentlemanly type of young man.'[27] In Killorglin, likewise, it was unthinkable that the local Volunteers be held accountable for a number of thefts in the parish, which occurred rather peculiarly during a series of raids. 'Whoever done it,' said Jamsey Moynihan, the local shoemaker, 'it wasn't the Sinn Féiners. There's plenty of lads about who'd take the guns right enough, but only blackguards would take the money!'[28] Those 'lads' were, in the words of the Reverend M.D. Forrest, 'the glory of Ireland: the most virtuous and chivalrous young men that the world (could) hope to produce'.[29]

The Volunteers also impressed and earned the respect of a number of loyalists in the county. They were efficient in their new role as policemen though, as one leading loyalist discovered, the policing did not come without its price.[30] According to Arthur Vincent of Muckross House:

*'A Rank and File of Bogtrotters and Cannibal Natives'*

In these disturbed times, it is only to be expected that in country districts here and there a gang of ill-doers should arise who are out for what they can get. The Volunteers in my district are the people we owners of property look to for assistance. In my district, they are doing their best to put down local robbing of orchards and to the Volunteers, I am personally indebted.[31]

High praise for the Volunteers. However, as Vincent also pointed out, while the local IRA worked to ensure that the Muckross orchards were not interfered with, their chief of police was allegedly out poaching his deer.

Popular recollection of the rebels has always been founded on the more thrilling IRA exploits such as the Headford ambush in March 1921 or the Ballymacandy ambush in May of that same year, but it does not follow that the rebel heroes depicted were representative of the typical Volunteer operating in the county at this time. 'Don't anyone ever think that there were Supermen in the 1916-1921 period,' warned Dan Mulvihill. 'There were no Supermen among us, we never had any!'[32] The Rt Hon Mr Vincent was not the only one to realise this, but 'fear of the consequences', as one irate curate put it in August 1921, meant that 'the people in general (were) afraid to complain' of inappropriate behaviour by local IRA companies.[33]

'You are a "scunk" of the first order which you are proving all along during your career over this way for the past year!' wrote a Catholic priest to Thomas Clifford, the Officer in Command (O/C) of the Ardfert Battalion, on hearing that the commandant had failed to lift a boycott on 'a poor widow and her orphans'.[34] Clifford managed to defend his actions to Richard Mulcahy, the Chief of Staff,

47

mainly because Mulcahy had been warned by that stage to treat the accusations of any member of the Kerry clergy with a good degree of caution. It appears, however, that the priest may not have been too far wrong in his judgement of the commandant who was later dismissed by his brigade officer for 'several irregularities and confiscation of finance'.[35] In the neighbouring parish of Lixnaw, likewise, Liam Lynch had to force the resignation of Commandant Thomas Kennelly, who was described as having 'brought the army to wholesale disrespect in his district'.[36] Meanwhile in Causeway, reports reached General Headquarters that the commandant there, a man named Connor, was 'deceiving his superior officers' and had appointed his brother as vice-commandant 'in order that they could deceive and blindfold the people'. 'First of all,' wrote the anonymous informer, 'over ninety men in the company are paying 6s a week, next goes the White Cross money, then the gate collections.'[37]

Reports about the IRA in the Kilflynn area were highlighted by a letter, this time from a solicitor called J.D. O'Connell, who informed General Headquarters (GHQ) that the goods seized by the Volunteers under the Belfast boycott were in turn being 'distributed to certain ladyfriends' of members of the company.[38] Similarly, Volunteers from the Newtownsandes Company were accused of crossing the border into Limerick and thieving from the locals there,[39] while in Ballymacelligott the two resident curates begged the Chief of Staff to dispatch a group of officers 'to investigate the whole state of discipline and conduct in the local company IRA'. According to Fr McDonnell, the local Volunteers had forcibly entered the home of one of their parishioners and held 'a dance until morning'.

A barrel of stout formed part of the entertainment, the greenhouse was broken into and the contents rifled, apples were taken off the trees and the gardens generally trampled all over. Two lockfast gates were fired … There are several other incidents that should be investigated, but it would be impossible to give a full account of the state of affairs. [40]

The brigade officers later dismissed any suggestion of misconduct on the part of the Volunteers in their area insisting that 'the Ballymacelligott Company (could) always rely on having plenty of people in their area to misrepresent their actions'.[41] The local community was taking every opportunity to 'cast as much mud as possible' at the company and its officers. Rumours were spread in the area that IRA officer and local creamery manager John Byrne, on the run since early 1920, had 'swindled' the Creamery Society members and fled with the money. Could this have contributed to the bad feeling towards the local IRA? Reports showed that the farmers of the area paid little attention to the rumour and even if it were true it is difficult to imagine how the action of one IRA man could have prompted such a wave of public indignation against the entire Volunteer body. Yet, according to Fr McDonnell, the local inhabitants were tired of the 'unruly' behaviour of the local Volunteer company, which was reputedly 'not left wanting in bad respect', and they approached the local clergy to make representation for them to IRA Headquarters.

Concern at the 'gross irregularities' occurring within the Volunteer units of the county was at every turn being talked about in any case. Liam Lynch, who assumed control of the 1st Southern Division in the spring of 1921, was immediately struck by the 'indiscipline' and 'complete lack of organisation,' particularly in north

Kerry. According to Lynch, the indiscipline needed 'to be put down at once' in order 'to save the honour of the Army in the area'.[42] Responsibility for the control and discipline of each Volunteer unit lay fundamentally with the battalion officers. The inability of the No. 1 Brigade Staff to satisfactorily check offending officers, or even doubt the conduct of Volunteer units, was therefore a factor in allowing such 'irregularities' to continue in the area. Active IRA officers attempted to excuse the apathy of the brigade staff during this period by attesting to the particularly large area under brigade control and to the difficulty of maintaining close contact with every IRA unit due to damaged communication lines and the concentration of British military activity.[43]

It appears, however, from the reports, that Paddy Cahill, the brigade's commanding officer, and his men may not have been entirely innocent of the accusations levelled against them by Headquarters. 'Under no circumstances could I recommend that Cahill be given brigade rank,' stated Liam Lynch in October 1920. 'I am anxious to have him attached to the staff as an assistant or otherwise as this I know would generally help the situation!'[44] 'How far Cahill would have utilised this staff I have my doubts,' was the reply of one inspector who had visited the Kerry camp. 'My view is that he prefers to act himself without consultation with any staff. Neither the brigade Vice-Commandant or Adjutant were ever continually in touch with him,' he despaired. 'There was too frequently little or no co-operation between battalions, the result being to cause an amount of ill-will and in some cases actual clashing of interests.'[45]

Cahill, on the run, according to Richard Mulcahy, had 'taken his column up Sliabh Mís and stayed there.'[46] There, in the view of another, they 'devoted their energies to eating, sleeping and general

*'A Rank and File of Bogtrotters and Cannibal Natives'*

amusement'.⁴⁷ 'They were fed like gamecocks by the people around who were all small farmers and poor,' stated rebel veteran Johnny Connors; and 'they used to send around to 200-300 farms for potatoes, milk, etc,'⁴⁸ according to Bertie Scully, an activist in Glenbeigh. The more vigilant Kerry No. 2 brigade appears to have been more informed of happenings in its area. This helped to deter misconduct among the rank and file Volunteers. It was still known to go on, however.

When Edmund Griffin, a small farmer from Cordal, Castleisland, challenged a £4 levy imposed on him by the local IRA company in June 1921, he soon regretted it. His son was taken down a by-road where a number of Volunteers 'took hold of each of his arms and threatened to shoot him'. Some days later, 'a large body of Volunteers surrounded (his) house. Over 100, under the order of Michael O'Leary, their captain, assaulted the place', taking the horse, harness, cattle and even the bicycle which 'Mrs Griffin and her daughters struggled to keep'. According to the parish priest, the local population was sickened by the act. Griffin, after all, had been one of the first to assist D.M. McCarthy, another IRA officer in the area, by sending 'a load of hay and horse to help out' when McCarthy's outhouses and hay were burned by Crown forces the previous February.⁴⁹ In a separate incident, O'Leary's name was linked to an order to formally acquit four Volunteers, court-martialled on good testimony for the robbery of Thomas Begley, a Knocknagoshel man, in April 1920. 'Men came to our house one night and asked my father for money', stated Begley's twelve-year-old son: 'He said he would not give it to them and when he said that one of them came over and struck him with a gun.' 'Two of them covered me and my wife with guns,' continued his father:

Barrett (one of the Volunteers) began searching in the corner of the room and out of a teapot took a five pound note and he put it into his pocket. In a few minutes he came up again and said boldly that he was looking for the money Dillane paid to (me) the evening before. I denied having the money in the house. Murphy and Moynihan had me covered with guns at the time. I was struck again in the mouth with the gun and Barrett then said they came for the money and would not go without it. Fearing they would kill me I told my wife to give them the money. They told me when going away not to say one word about it and not tell anyone or they would call again.[50]

Begley certainly found himself in a very frustrating position with the acquittal. The rules were clearly bent to suit the fighting men, but this was wartime, and good fighting men were needed as was money.

The intention of Tom Daly, O/C of the Listry Battalion, to keep 'enemy money for arming and equipping (his) army', went to show that lapses in good conduct resulted as much from patriotic regard as from a seeming lack of it. 'If we hold it,' wrote Daly excitedly, following the seizure of almost £100 in government salaries and £80 worth of old-age pensions, 'the British will send on further amounts to the employees.'[51] 'You will have every penny of this returned,' replied Michael Collins, the Adjutant-General. 'The fact that it is the property of the enemy government does not make it less binding on us to preserve our reputation. Nothing would do more to break this than such an act.'[52] Numerous references in the police files to the disappearance of mail throughout the 1920-1 period indicates that the Kerry battalions were past caring about orders from GHQ regarding their precious 'reputation'. The more serious republicans would not intentionally set out to disobey a direct order from GHQ but, in the event of there being a difference of opinion, the local way of doing things invariably won out. Men like Daly, who believed they were justified in taking money to fund their war with Britain, would not have made the same mistake twice in terms of alerting GHQ. Besides, money would not have been the main reason for taking the mail. Above all, the post provided the fighting men with information on the goings on in an area and so it was a valuable source of intelligence. GHQ was at a disadvantage, with even the most influential officers unable to make much of an impact on the devil-may-care attitude within the local columns.

Almost all areas of the county also had their share of 'rough riders'. They were guilty of commandeering goods and motorcars for what they called 'legitimate IRA purposes'. According to Jeremiah Murphy:

> These actions were necessary for our survival ... the seizure of private property was covered by an order from Headquarters as long as we issued a receipt for the goods. I drove Den Reen and Con Moynihan on the motorcycle to collect cigarettes and escaped a swipe of a tongs from a local shopkeeper as she protested at our commandeering of her property.[53]

The GHQ 'order' was abused and often used as a cover for taking goods that were not necessities, and reports show that this was common practice. Prominent IRA officers in the Ballybunion area were accused of commandeering a motorcycle and using 'the machine for joyriding',[54] Further southwards in Sneem, a local hotel owner complained to Liam Lynch that she had spent the last four months awaiting the return of her 'lorries', which as far as she could see 'had been used only to amuse people'.[55]

One irate bicycle owner from Brosna took it upon himself to write to 'President de Valera' when his bicycle was taken by the IRA of the parish 'under wrongful and aggravating circumstances'. 'Those dastards,' he cried, 'should not have taken any man's bicycle much less than that of a US citizen, save by consent.'[56] Sister Philomena McCarthy, writing of her experiences as a child in Kenmare during the War of Independence, remembered how Tom Scarteen O'Connor, 'in Norfolk jacket and elegant riding breeches accompanied by Danny Quill of Gort Luachrea and two other Volunteers', spent the summer of 1921 driving around 'in Lord Kenmare's high trap with a beautiful horse which they had commandeered some time before.'[57] 'We were in the Brigade Column then and we were, as we thought, a cut above the local fellows,' confessed Johnny Connors, also active in the Kerry No. 2 area:

> If we went into a brigade area, the local man would take you to your billet and your bed and everything was ready for you. For movement there was a convoy of ponies and traps and we used three times the amount we required.[58]

In some cases, however, the county's Volunteers set their sights on even greater spoils or, as one county court judge accused, availed of 'the abnormal condition of things to do all the fleecing they (could)'.[59]

One landowner near Tralee was kidnapped and compelled to sign away some 40 acres of land 'at the point of a revolver'.[60] Meanwhile, in Castleisland, auctioneers were 'asked' by local IRA officers 'to forego their auctioneering business and allow it to pass into the hands of a deserving Volunteer', since they were, in the

*'A Rank and File of Bogtrotters and Cannibal Natives'*

opinion of one officer, 'all men who could easily afford to give up this branch of their business'.[61] Respect or indeed fear of the IRA was such that few would refuse them any request and this was something that the men, both active and inactive, exploited and used to their own advantage. 'You could not prevent (them),' explained Lady Gordon, 'for (they) were armed and you were not.'[62]

Veterans, however, reject the suggestion that their conduct was in any way underhand. They insist that attacks were directed only against known enemies of the Republic and were, for the most part, deserved. An examination of the sources paint a different picture. Rebel outrages were sometimes found to be indiscriminate, where a person could just as easily be targeted for his assets as for his political principles.

It is to the rebels' credit, however, that there were not too many instances of serious wrongdoing or crime. The rebels were young, often impetuous and immature, but their rearing as 'honest sons', and 'good Catholics' meant that the level of serious crime against local communities was kept to a minimum. A pamphlet on the Tan War Operations issued by the Sinn Féin Publicity Department in the 1980s did highlight a number of incidences that were not typical of the Kerry boys. In March 1921 Martin Daly, a 60-year-old farmer, was shot dead near Tralee. The pamphlet told of how he had been living in fear since he handed over a Sinn Féin Summons to the military. Evidence showed that 'there were numerous injuries to the body. The face was peppered with small shot and the jaw was broken. Some ribs were broken and a shot had passed through the lung'. The shooting of Sir Arthur Vicars, Listowel, was also an unwarranted killing. Vicars was considered to be a fairly harmless character and was probably shot for his land. His home, Kilmorna House, was set on fire by the rebels, totally destroying its contents, worth thousands of pounds, and a wealth of historically irreplaceable objects. That in itself was a mindless act of blackguarding. These instances on the part of the rebels were very much the exception, however.[63]

The Volunteers were for the most part 'plain' people, hard-working and 'highly respectable'.[64] Con Casey remarked, they 'came from what you would call the lower middle class ... not too much to lose that they might be scared of being involved'.[65] Farmers' sons were generally quite active within the movement. The RIC nearly always detected a lull in rebel activity at ploughing or harvest time. 'Fifty-seven outrages were committed during the month as compared with eighty during the previous month,' announced County Inspector Gerity in June 1920. 'The decrease is due to the season of the year, the short nights and the fact that the men are employed at agriculture.'[66] Tom MacEllistrim could recall being intercepted by scouts while on his way to the bog with his workmen, and in mid-Kerry drill manoeuvres rarely started before seven in the evening on account of the milking.[67]

However, the farmers' sons were by no means predominant in the movement. Closer examination of Volunteer backgrounds reveals that both the skilled and semi-skilled sectors were also strongly represented within the ranks. In east Kerry, for example, the strength of the skilled workers within the early Sinn Féin movement was such that the locals called it 'The Tailor's Club'.[68] In Tralee, Con Casey recalled that C Company, in the middle of the town, was composed primarily of drapers, grocers and clerks,[69] while it was 'a few of the tailors' in the town of Listowel who first urged Ed Quirke to go along to the meetings.[70] A great number of the 'fishing craft' from Dingle and Valentia were, according to one county inspector, 'entirely manned by

Sinn Féiners'.[71] (Sinn Féiners and IRA men, in the eyes of some RIC men, being one and the same in County Kerry at this time).[72] A sample of 117 rank-and-file Volunteers active during the 1919-21 campaign shows that skilled workers accounted on the whole for 21 per cent, while 44 per cent were farmers' sons.[73] Of the remaining 35 per cent, 17 per cent were unskilled workers, including shop assistants and general labourers, but with agricultural labourers accounting for well over half of this figure. Most of the 'professionals' who made up the remainder in the sample were teachers, who, like many of the grocers' assistants categorised in the unskilled group, would have originally come from a farming background.

| | |
|---|---|
| *Farmers* | 56 |
| Skilled | 17 |
| Unskilled/ Semi-skilled | 7 |
| Agricult. Labourers | 14 |
| Profession | 23 |

(Occupations of County Kerry IRA Rank in File 1918-21*)

| | |
|---|---|
| *Farmers* | 18 |
| Skilled | 16 |
| Unskilled/ Semi-Skilled | 8 |
| Agricult.. Labourers | 2 |
| Profession/ Business | 22 |
| Ex-RIC/Army | 5 |

(Occupations of Co. Kerry IRA leaders 1918-21**)

* / **(Names and backgrounds for both samples were taken from *The Kerryman, Killarney Echo*; reports to the CMA re Infringement of Defence of the Realm Regulations, PROL, CO 904/103-12; veteran statements and accounts)

The samples are based on noted rebels who came to official attention during 1919-21 and may not prove to be a completely accurate representation of the full membership. It is still hugely significant, however, in that it shows that all the Volunteers considered were involved in some form of gainful employment and not, as was the loyalist view of things, 'young idlers about the street corners who (preferred) mischief to work'.

With regard to the occupations of 76 IRA officers, on the other hand, 28 per cent were classed as 'professionals' with the majority falling under the category of teachers, accountants, engineers or men with a university education. A good education was, for GHQ, a prerequisite for any type of command.[74] According to John Joe Sheehy, the men would have looked on any fellow who had been to college as 'well-up'[75] and would have been better inclined to accept his leadership as a result. Significantly, the percentage of unskilled or semi-skilled workers was reasonably high at 13 per cent, with skilled workers accounting for 20 per cent of all officers in the sample. Farmers' sons made up the difference apart from the few ex-RIC or army men. It is also interesting to note that just 23 of the 65 officers considered in the sample were active in 1916. This suggests that many of the older officers, or those married and with families, opted out in favour of the younger men when the going got tough. Take, for example, the case of Jeremiah O'Connell, the officer in command of the Cahirciveen Battalion in 1916. By 1919, he had resigned from his position, being a married man with seven children.[76] This was not always the case, however. Officials at GHQ had their own work cut out for them in late 1921 when trying to remove officers who were 'too old' and altogether 'too slow' for the job in hand.[77]

Every man had a different motive for joining the movement and

## 'A Rank and File of Bogtrotters and Cannibal Natives'

similarly had different expectations. There are indications, certainly, that the more prominent rebels in the county were intensely nationalistic.[78] Other statements show that most IRA men boasted only 'enough knowledge of history and tradition to show them why they should be involved'.[79] Political aspirations do not appear to have been particularly high in the priorities of the Ballydesmond corps, for instance. In 1917 many of them were still unable to pronounce the name 'de Valera'.[80] Ed Quirke knew some lads in Listowel who became involved with the movement only 'because it seemed the right thing to do at the time', while others, like Dan Mulvihill, joined up merely for 'kicks'.[81] Mulvihill was 'on the run by choice' and, as one of his accounts showed, lived only for the thrill of a fight:

> We wounded three of them, none seriously, but we were very happy going home we had been under fire. I think I got a greater kick out of that than anything else in the Tan time. It was grand to be young and on the run in Glencar that summer of 1920.

Brian O'Grady also attributed the transformation of the Ballylongford company to the 'sensation' created following a series of raids in the parish. Thereafter, 'when we went to the hall it was packed and excitement also prevailed there, and a good few made application to join the IRA.'[82] The element of danger certainly provided an impetus for the more adventurous to join the movement. Yet, ironically, the increase in militant activity later on was a far more significant factor in damaging the overall membership. Out of an estimated 4,057 Volunteers on the Kerry No. 1 battalion rolls in July 1921, only 1,996, or less than half, was considered 'reliable'. The number who regularly appeared on parade was comparatively higher at 3,014 with all seven battalions averaging a turnout of at least 77 per cent. This figure, while encouraging, does not necessarily reflect the fighting power available. Drill manoeuvres in no way endangered the lives of the men involved and men were more likely to absent themselves from actual fighting.

The 2nd Battalion at Ardfert, despite having 655 men out on parade at any given time, considered only 342 of its men reliable while in the Dingle battalion, on the other side of the brigade area, 280 or less than half of the 581-strong battalion showed interest. These figures, arguably, could be even lower if one takes seriously Brian O'Grady's assertion that only five or six from each company participated in any meaningful way during the conflict. The company roll from his own area, Ballylongford, points to just 20 out of a possible 60 showing any potential. The Glencar company, moreover, despite being part of 'a small Republic', had 50 men affiliated with less than 30 active in the area, while in Tarbert six men from a 60-strong company were left to carry on the war against the British.[83]

There were quite a number of 'wannabe' individuals within the Volunteers at the time. These would have identified with Christy O'Grady, the young Tralee scout, who went and bought a trenchcoat for £2.15 perhaps so that he could look the part.[84] They were the kind who, like O'Grady, stood in awe of 'chaps in full IRA uniform' who stayed the night at his mother's hotel.[85] Mainstream republican motives for joining included wiles of youth as much as a sense of obligation to the Republic. In contrast to die-hard nationalists like Thomas Ashe and Austin Stack, many were 'moderate men'[86] who went in during the conscription scare and it was largely a matter of chance if they emerged as fighters. The county was full of Volunteers with 'lovely command words'. Moderates 'addicted to peaceable drilling on fine nights' so long as it did not interfere with the 'substantial deposit in the savings bank', or the hanger-on type like the publican from Ballydonoghue who was good for marching and looking the part.[87]

Battalion rolls indicate that Billy Mullins' view of the Kerry rebels as 'a real guerrilla fighting firm' was somewhat overstated. Further examination is required before we can conclude that the fighting men of Kerry were, in the words of one outsider, 'a mob', who were badly trained, poorly armed and held back by ineffective officers.[88] It has been shown, however, that the general type of rebel that emerged in Kerry was a combination of youth, respectability and vision. Their actions frequently were not characteristic of their class, but these were not typical times. It is fair to say that the majority rarely lost sight of the cause for which they were fighting and a vision of independence that was promised should they succeed.

# 4

# THE WILL OF THE PEOPLE OR THE DESIRE OF A FEW?

IRA GENERAL Headquarters (GHQ) was not in a position to deal with Volunteer misconduct until the Truce. The county's units were fiercely independent and, when it came to discipline, GHQ had to tread carefully. However, by the time of the Truce, the level of complaints against the Volunteers in Kerry was worryingly high and GHQ could not continue to let it go unchecked. The fact that grievances were brought to Dublin points to a breakdown in communication, with people getting little satisfaction from local officers when it came to dealing with offenders. A genuine fear of the consequences meant that many were reluctant to complain openly; the last thing a family wanted was for the local company to become aware of any griping.

RIC reports also suggest that the number of outrages was much higher than those communicated, yet the threat of violence and the fear of being 'labelled' prevented many from disclosing details of the assaults. In fact, while the British authorities had records of attacks

*The Will of the People or the Desire of a Few?*

and the motives of the men involved, it was rare for the victims to give the names of their assailants. 'People not falling into line with the IRA are either shot or threatened with death,' wrote one county inspector in June 1921, and even though 'the country farmers and village shopkeepers' were 'heartily sick' of them, 'they dared not openly complain.'[1] 'Kerry continues in a disturbed state', was the observation of another inspector the previous July. He continued:

> Only 37 outrages, it is true, were reported as compared with 57 during the preceding month, but many of them were very serious and a large number never reached the ears of the police at all. I consider that the decrease indicates no improvement in the state of the area, but rather points to the fact that the power of Sinn Féin is so generally acknowledged that it is unnecessary to resort to outrage.[2]

An intelligence officer with the Second Battalion Loyal Regiment in the county gave an account of an assault on a family in the Listowel area:

> A number of men rushed the house of Miss Dillon, Meen, six miles from Listowel. They made her brothers Dan, Con and John dress up and go out with them. They killed a dog and also drove off seven cows. This family has no connection with Sinn Féin. They have two brothers with the RIC, one in Macroom and the other in Galway (yet) the brothers refused to make a statement after their release and Miss Dillon refused to sign her statement ... (remarking) 'I may be killed if I said anything'.[3]

A man in the Killarney area had much the same response for the police when he withdrew a claim against his local IRA company on the reckoning that 'life (was) too sweet'.[4]

The traditional assertion that civilians throughout the country gave unqualified support to their fighting men might well be considered in the light of such information. 'The people were very good all through the county,' assured Johnny Connors, and 'would be jealous if you didn't stay at their particular house!'[5] It seems that perceived opponents of the IRA bore the brunt of Volunteer retribution. No family was deliberately going to bring the wrath of their local company down on them, when some of their more obstinate neighbours awoke at times to find outhouses burned, cattle maimed or graves dug outside their doors. Men in Cahirciveen who refused to hand over bicycles to the IRA had their tyres slashed and wheels buckled.[6] A woman called Brosnan from Castleisland had her pony trap seized by the local company 'as punishment for her general hostility to the movement,'[7] while rebel veteran, John Joe Rice, recalled years later how the parish priest of Kenmare had his bullock taken 'for sermons he preached against us'.[8] IRA officers threatened vengeance in the Killarney area when locals invited a number of British military officers to join them on a day's hunting. The leaders of the hunt were warned that unless all association with the military ceased, the dogs would be poisoned and the hunting banned.[9]

Likewise, in Cahirdaniel, suspected British sympathisers could expect to be callously dealt with. In March 1920, Cornelius Kelly, the caretaker of the local courthouse, was shot dead by six masked men in front of his wife and child; he was storing a number of police bicycles that were left after the RIC withdrew from the barrack.[10] In Castlegregory the following month, the body of Patrick Foley, an ex-

*The Will of the People or the Desire of a Few?*

soldier and newly-appointed member of the RIC, was found in a creamery yard, his body 'shattered with bullets'. The inquest showed 26 gunshot wounds to his body, seven in the centre of his chest. According to the medical evidence, any of the chest wounds could have caused death.[11] Foley was related to Tim Kennedy, a leading activist in the county, and was a cousin of Paddy Cahill, officer in command of the Kerry No. 1 Brigade. They had discovered that Foley was supplying the police with information against them and could not be seen to let it continue.[12] Why use seven bullets though when one would have sufficed? After all, ammunition was not that plentiful. Whoever killed Foley was intent on sending a message to the wider community. It is clear that the brutality was meant to underline a warning against all IRA enemies and family was no exception.[12] His killing was used as an example of that which could befall any opponent of the cause, public or private.

Veteran republicans were aware of 'real blackguards' operating within the Volunteers during this period.[13] This type was well known to Susie Casey, wife of Con Casey. She recalled the 'tough bunch' of boys who would arrive from Ballymacelligott to their house in Firies and prove 'too drunk to be reasonable!'[14] The Volunteers from the Cork/Kerry border, meanwhile, had a reputation for being 'a tough crowd'. At Ballylongford, a doctor sent to a camp to attend to two injured men never before encountered such an 'unholy crowd'. '(He) thought they would shoot him', said IRA man Denis Quill, and was anxious to get out of the camp, 'such was the fooling with their guns!'[15]

Many respectable republicans in the county, however, privately saw the need for a bit of 'blackguarding' in order to enforce decrees. During 1921, for example, as organised opposition to the payment of Council rates strengthened, Volunteer police, according to John Brassil of Ballylongford Farmers' Association, started 'raiding decent houses at unreasonable hours to the terror of the inmates' in an effort to frighten defaulters into paying.[16] The rates had continued to soar throughout 1920 as the number of malicious injury claims increased.[17] The British government had ceased all annual payments to the Council by May and by the end of the year the Farmers' Unions of the county had joined the masses of objectors. In March 1921 only seven out of 29 collectors from the county had fully closed their rate collections.[18] 'Reports are at hand,' wrote one Kerry inspector, 'of organised opposition to paying rates from Ballylongford, Kilgarvin, Killorglin.' An IRA officer warned that 'it has spread from Tarbert to Ballylongford, from there to Asdee and now it is spreading to Ballybunion'. His solution was plainly put:

> I could easily supply twenty men off my company to travel to Newtown or Duagh district, say, while they in turn could do the same and you know yourself, strangers have a greater effect in this thing than any others. If a few of the ringleaders were kidnapped, or something that way, it would have effect.[19]

This bit of 'blackguarding' evidently worked and Denis Quill, an IRA man and representative of the Sinn Féin Court at Listowel, was able to assure Austin Stack by November that the 'gang' was being 'broken up'. This was on account of arrests and cattle-seizures by the Volunteer police and that 'those who have had to pay costs now are very sorry that they ever allowed civil bills to go out against them.'[20] Staunch friends 'of the enemy during the critical stages' was how Florence O'Donoghue saw these types.[21] IRA men had a tendency to describe such perceived enemies as a 'privileged' or 'polished type', similar to a spy shot outside Rathkeale found to be 'wearing silk underclothes'.[22] C.H. Bretherton had another theory:

> At no time could the Sinn Féin rebellion be regarded as a rising of the Irish people. The word Republic meant nothing to them … (they) watched the contest with singular detachment, unwilling to side with the rebels yet in sympathy with them afraid to side with the British.[23]

'They appeared', opined Frederick Palmer on 11 March 1922 in the *New York Evening Post*, 'to be more concerned over the price of butter and eggs' and desired only a 'return to order'.[24] Bretherton, in particular, was an ardent critic of the IRA.[25] However, neither writer seems to have been too far wide of the mark in their observation of the ordinary man and his relations with the IRA. In a letter to a friend in May 1921, Lady Albinia Broderick wrote:

> If ten years ago anyone had told me that we could live through what we are living through now, I imagine that one would have thought him a sheer lunatic. It will interest you to hear how things are with us. South Kerry, West Kerry, and the greater part of East Kerry have neither trains nor posts. Everything in the way of provisioning must be done by boat and common car. In occasional places lorries can run. But between want of permits, cut roads, broken bridges and felled trees, even that means of locomotion is more than difficult. And to that, this last week an order is out forbidding the use of bicycles without a permit, which most people would be refused even if their principles

allowed them to ask for one; and the fact that these lovely summer evenings, every soul in Tralee and for three miles outside must be indoors by nine o'clock and you may begin to form a faint conception of the general foundations of our life.[26]

Another writer in north Kerry spoke of 'a deliberate attempt to harm and terrorise a large district which (had) been a model community for good order'.[27] The people wanted a return to order but while the IRA remained abroad and dangerous, the severity of British reprisal action would continue.

The independence fighters were blamed for adding to the people's dilemma. John O'Connor, himself a leading republican supporter from Rathmore, felt compelled to write to his superiors and 'confess the state of utter demoralisation into which Kerry has fallen' as a result of IRA shortcomings.[28] In December 1921, Bartholomew Dillane, a farmer from Cahirciveen, described in a letter addressed to the Secretary of Dáil Éireann how a group of Volunteers commandeered a sheep worth £3 while they were camped on his land. 'I have supported the movement in every possible way,' he cried. 'I gave subscriptions towards the Dáil for rifles. I have not been compensated nor see no likelihood of being so, I cannot afford to give so much.'[29] His neighbour, Patrick Walsh, from Emulaghmore, had a similar complaint, and he showed even less enthusiasm for the cause as he demanded to be reimbursed for a loan given to the local Volunteers:

I paid the sum of £1 towards rifles towards the Volunteers. So did every other household. I have supported the movement in every way. They were supported in their camps by the country people. I wish to know if the £1 paid was legal and I want to claim it now.[30]

*The Will of the People or the Desire of a Few?*

Both Dillane and Walsh were clearly at pains to indicate that neither they nor their neighbours parted willingly with their possessions. Why then continue contributing to the cause when they were, as Dillane maintained, unable to afford it? Perhaps the attitude of these men was an exception? Or, perhaps, they could not refuse? It is remarkable to see how the people managed to keep contributing to an organisation when employment in the area was 'practically nil', with acute food shortages also reported as a result of the failed potato crop the previous year.[31]

Liam Lynch reported in May 1921 that the Cahirciveen area was in a state of crisis and on the brink of starvation, due to a military blockade by the British after an ambush at Glenbeigh.

The conditions of the civil population in the Kerry No. 3 Brigade area were very serious. It was found that a very real possibility of famine existed if something was not done to alleviate the distress.[32] Money was scarce but the rebels in the area continued to receive support. This is not to say that assistance was always forced from the people. Some fighters were careful about who they approached since in most areas there were only a half-dozen houses that could really be considered 'safe'.[33] The people of Glencar appear to have been the exception in this regard, creating for themselves 'a small Republic' where the rebels could reputedly find shelter in almost any house. 'There were a couple of dozen safe houses,' reckoned Dan Mulvihill, but then, 'the people were out on their own. They loved to have fellows on the run amongst them and they went out of their way to find things to do for them.'[34] In Kilcummin, Sheila Humpheries heard that 'every house as far as the eye (could) see' had put men up.[35] Tom MacEllistrim, who roamed with the brigade column in the Kerry No. 2 area, also appears to have encountered a reliable sort in his area. 'The RIC tried to catch us in every way they could,' he triumphed, 'but they failed for if they had a raid on we'd have a message about it within ten minutes.' The inhabitants of Tralee town were well known for assisting 'the rebels and (thwarting) the authorities in their efforts to trace them',[36] and were trusted enough by MacEllistrim and Jack Cronin to 'stroll into Tralee where (they would) have a few drinks'.[37]

Other active Volunteers give a very different impression of 'the town crowd'. According to Bertie Scully, they were generally 'no good' and their homes were 'dens of informers'.[38] This distrust reflected what Peter Hart has called the 'enduring divide between town and country'.[39] The same distinctions existed in Kerry, but were not as obvious due to the rural nature of its community. There are, nonetheless, numerous examples of this class tension, particularly in the diary of one Tralee scout, Christopher O'Grady. There are references to the 'poor countrys' who came to do their business in the town.[40] May Dalaigh, herself born and reared on a farm in Firies, also hinted at the distinction that existed between town and country folk at this time. 'They thought we were so green that we would not notice a horse and cart going through the yard with logs to make a dug-out,' she recalled of John Joe Sheehy and his men, rebels from Tralee town, who had stayed on the farm for a time in early 1922. 'That (was) their idea of country people. I used to say to John Joe, "Kerry 1 had to run to Kerry 2 for shelter". He did not like that!'[41]

Class prejudice aside, the evidence shows that the more wary of the county's Volunteers were probably right about the local 'town crowd' when they described them as fair-weather republicans. The officer in command of the Kerry No. 2 Brigade blamed the failure of an attack on Castleisland barracks in July 1921 on the suspected treachery of the townspeople. 'We had to try to keep out of the town until the last minute,' he explained, 'for if the inhabitants were aware of our presence the military would be made aware of it also.'[42] Likewise, a planned attack on a barracks between Castleisland and Knocknagoshel had to be abandoned when the authorities got, what Johnny Connors called, 'a tip-off' when coming through Knocknagoshel. 'The men were going to sack the town that night, but it was called off. We were going to carry it out as a reprisal.'[43] Betrayal by Castlemaine villagers, similarly, meant that the local column was forced to change its position at Ballymacandy in May 1921. According to Dan Mulvihill:

> We went to the north of the village and there was no suitable position there ... so we came on through the village realising that the village was a more dangerous problem than the Tans. We knew they would stop for a drink and would be told we were out. We went on to Jack Flynn's gate and made our decision there. We decided to ambush them where there was no position, as they would be told we were ahead.[44]

In Killorglin town, six miles on, the inhabitants did not appear to have been much better. They were 'no good' in the opinion of Bertie Scully. 'We couldn't get much information out of it,' agreed Tom O'Connor, 'the AOH had been too strong (and) O'Donnell a former MP had a great hold on them'. Even the Killorglin rebels were at times considered a disgrace to the ranks. MacEllistrim, sent to the town on the day before the truce to plan an attack on the barracks, was forced to withdraw as the scouts were 'no good' and the men lacked the nerve to start the fight. 'The barracks was in the centre of the town with civilian houses on either side of it,' remembered MacEllistrim. 'The people had to be warned. We had as much gun powder as would have blown the barracks to pieces but the men were unwilling to warn the civilians so I took responsibility for it and called off the job.'[45]

MacEllistrim was not the only one to experience difficulty with IRA members from the towns. Ernie O'Malley looked on most of the town recruits as poor nationalists that made only second-rate fighters. 'Towns we could not count on,' he wrote, 'the men in the towns were not up to requisite standards.'[46] Opposition by businessmen, and other 'men of stake', to the Volunteers definitely undermined the development of the movement in the towns. Most businessmen wanted nothing to do with a movement that had 'no foundation' and was 'all rubbish'. In Killorglin town, the wayward son of one businessman was made swear himself out of a local Volunteer company in the presence of the RIC County Inspector.[47] Other 'stake in the country' men took their opposition even further, threatening known sympathisers with dismissal unless they broke their connection with republicanism.[48]

J.J. Barrett, the son of IRA activist Joe Barrett, has claimed also that 'there were few republican followers amongst the Tralee families who constituted the livestock buying industry'.

> Traditionally the pig and cattle business was run by families. They were usually fairly comfortably off, and would generally be establishment supporters ... When the Barretts entered that first fair after being released from the Internment Camps they were shunned 'as if we had the plague', my uncle Tommy Barrett told me.[49]

The growing strength of the Irish Transport and General Workers' Union during this period also affected the republican support base. 'Where it succeeds in country districts it is to the detriment of Sinn Féin as the members who join both put this organisation first,' was the opinion of County Inspector Heard.[50] In the towns where the number of union members was proportionately higher, Sinn Féin definitely suffered in terms of active support. However, RIC reports for the period indicate that Sinn Féin and the Volunteers were in a healthy state, with no decrease in membership, between September 1918 and February 1920, the time that the ITGWU was building up its membership. ITGWU figures continued to increase at a slower rate throughout 1920 and eventually levelled off in January 1921 at 2,760 members (see Table 1). This increase occurred without affecting republican membership figures, but it did damage Sinn Féin's influence. 'It (was) only the knowledge that it would affect their pockets and that they would not get general labour support which prevent(ed) them introducing Sinn Féin into their labour disputes,'[51] wrote Heard. When it came to prioritising a week's pay or the future of Ireland, many town rebels went for the less glorious option. Most did not have a farm or an education to fall back on, and the bottom line was that if they missed a day's work through drilling or ambushing they did not get paid. Volunteers had to live as much for the present as for the future.

In addition, the men from the towns did not have the traditions of moonlighting and land agitation that may have informed the behaviour of their rural compatriots. Agrarian and Fenian traditions were considered laudable components of a republican's upbringing and an important factor in their 'readiness to fight'.[52] John Joe Rice insisted, in fact, that in an area where there was a

|  |  | *Sinn Féin* |  | *Irish Vols* |  | *ITGWU* |  |
|---|---|---|---|---|---|---|---|
| Sept. | 1918 | 6,550 | 60 Clubs | 2,698 | 19 Clubs | 340 | 4 Clubs |
| Jan. | 1919 | 6,479 | (60) | 2,964 | (25) | 560 | (4) |
| March | 1919 | 6,524 | (61) | 2,963 | (25) | 1,529 | (13) |
| May | 1919 | 6,530 | (61) | 2,963 | (25) | 2,521 | (18) |
| August | 1919 | 6,524 | (61) | 2,963 | (25) | 2,712 | (20) |
| Jan. | 1920 | 6,531 | (61) | 2,963 | (25) | 2,725 | (19) |
| June | 1920 | 6,528 | (61) | 3,046 | (28) | 2,758 | (21) |
| Jan. | 1921 | 6,545 | (61) | 3,499 | (28) | 2,760 | (21) |
| April | 1921 | 6,543 | (61) | 3,099 | (28) | 2,760 | (21) |

Table 1: *Royal Irish Constabulary membership returns for organisations active, September 1918-April 1921*[53]

moonlighting tradition or a strong Fenian element, families could generally be relied upon.[54]

It should be borne in mind also that town-based IRA activists had less opportunities for attack due to the much larger concentration of troops in their areas and the fewer places for retreat.[55] Town fighters, as a result, were not typically as experienced or battle-hardened as their compatriots in the country. One cannot rule out the possibility either that close proximity to the chapel might have had its part to play in explaining the hesitancy or indeed the willingness of the IRA boys to fight. Most IRA veterans hotly deny that they ever allowed themselves to be intimidated by the local clergy, but given the strength of Catholic tradition in the county,[56] and the fact that most young rebels were either altar-boys or 'frequenters of the sacraments',[57] the attitude of the priests must have had some impact. The parish priest in Con Brosnan's area had enough influence over the local IRA to secure the release of two RIC men kidnapped following

*The Will of the People or the Desire of a Few?*

the killing of Eddie Carmody by Crown Forces in November 1920.[58] However, 'there were very few all right', in the view of John Joe Rice. Rice did mention Fr Kiely from Fossa who told him that the men could go to him at any time for confession. Yet in the same statement he described how Mick Reardon, an IRA captain in Kilgarvin, watched his men 'passed over one by one at the altar rails'. They were eventually forced back to their seats by a Fr Breen with the words, 'Communion is not for the likes of you'.[59] An officer with the Ballymacelligott Company sought advice from Richard Mulcahy on how to deal with the troublemaking Fr McDonnell, his parish priest. 'On one occasion,' wrote the distraught captain, 'he said that the name of Ballymac stunk in the nostrils of the people of Ireland and on another occasion, "What could the Volunteers do with their six little rifles against the British Army?"'[60] Archdeacon Marstall from Listowel, meanwhile, was described as 'the greatest imperialist of all time' and 'very bad during the Tan War' by IRA veteran Billy Mullins. Mullins believed that they were all 'just following in the footsteps of a previous Bishop who had stated from the pulpit that hell was not hot enough for the Fenians,'[61] 'Our dead were refused to be allowed in the churches,' stated Rice, 'but in some cases they were put into the churches in spite of them.'[62]

Such clergymen's lack of sympathy with the republican cause could lead to bitterness. For example, in a letter to his sister, one north Kerry man described how Fr Keane, a curate in Athea, could have prevented the murders of Paddy Dalton, Jerry Lyons and Patrick Walsh, the three men shot in a field at Gortaglanna by the Black and Tans in early May 1921.

'Here they were lost as Fr Keane passed by them on the road from Mass and never got off to try to help them, though one was near related to him. Everyone says if he got on to them the police would not have dared shoot them afterwards.'[63]

'Thank God, not all were of that mind,' stated Billy Mullins.[64] The priests of Ballylongford, according to Brian O'Grady, were very sympathetic to the local company. Fr Harty was president of the Sinn Féin Court in the area and his parish priest, Canon Harty, left his parishoners in no doubt of where his sympathies lay when following an IRA raid for guns in the area he told them from the pulpit:

> I am one who would not condemn them, because generations of our people have been fighting for that freedom for the last seven hundred years. The youth of today are more educated and I am sure they will be better disciplined and will have better facilities for training than they had years ago.[65]

The violence used by the British forces against the people also helped increase clerical support for the Volunteers. Even Cardinal Logue, the Catholic primate, condemned the action of the authorities as 'inexcusable'.

> They have turned loose on the country a horde of savages, some of them, if not many, are simply brigands, burglars and thieves. It is no longer a question of reprisals, it is a matter of laying waste the country.[66]

The priests of Kerry were not afraid to express their own political views and the public would have been guided by them. This would have worked to the advantage and disadvantage of IRA companies depending on which side of the political divide the local priest was on. It is worth questioning if opposition by priests to the armed struggle was derived from bad experiences with Volunteers in their parishes? The priest's house was one of the few safe places where a parishioner could talk openly about IRA wrongdoing. If the offence was bad enough they might even have had a letter of complaint written to someone in Dublin, or at the very least the bad name of the IRA read from the pulpit. Some Kerry priests could have been anti-IRA because of the IRA, and the priest's opinion counted for a lot and certainly impacted on public support for the movement. It is also worth noting that for the first time the unbridled authority of the Church was being challenged. The IRA as a group was not afraid to confront or stand up to the local priest. They were not going to run their war according to the priest's say and a local priest's objection to the IRA could have been founded on this as much as on moral issues. According to John Joe Rice, it was only within the glens that 'the attitude of the bishop and others had no effect on the people for (they) were good and solid'.[67] 'The glens were an independent fighting people',[68] 'fully in sympathy with the cause'.[69] They also had the added advantage of homes that were far removed from the constant preaching of the clergy.

# 5

# 'The IRA Mob'

I am quite satisfied that nearly all the battalion commandants believe that I did my best and as regards the local working of the Brigade, I am foolish enough to think that I have not been a failure. (Paddy Cahill, Officer in Command (O/C) Kerry No. 1 Brigade, to Richard Mulcahy, Chief of Staff, May 1921)[1]

DURING AN inspection tour of County Kerry in the early summer of 1921, Florence O'Donoghue, an officer on the staff of the 1st Southern Division, wrote in his letters home:

> Everywhere we saw signs of extraordinary efficiency and wonderful organisation ... on every vantage point above the road scouts were posted and we could see their messages passing from hill to hill to ensure our safety. At every crossroads a straight limbed country boy in his working clothes clicked his heels smartly and saluted as we went past.

In west Kerry, 'the same scouting arrangements impressed' and preparations for an engagement were, in O'Donoghue's view, nothing if not 'cool and unhurried'. 'Men seeing that everything is in order wait with apparent unconcern, chatting as usual, but with every sense alert; they have a self-confidence and a courage which is indeed heroic.'[2] The visit was, by Dan Mulvihill's account, the 'best guarded ever to be held in Kerry', with scouts within sight of each other all the way to Tralee, Killarney, Killorglin and Farranfore'.[3]

O'Donoghue's impression of the Kerry IRA was not one shared by General Headquarters (GHQ) at that time; indeed, Liam Lynch had been complaining of 'gross' inefficiency in the county ever since his appointment to the 1st Southern Division in April 1921.[4] As late as October 1921 GHQ still had not 'a full idea of the discredit' the army was brought to 'in some areas'.[5] Which version is closest to the truth? The conventional image of the Kerry rebel is apparently strengthened by O'Donoghue's findings, but perhaps what he encountered was simply an efficient effort by the locals to impress a senior officer?

GHQ was contemplating a shake-up in the brigade leadership and it could be that the Kerry chiefs were attempting to convince senior officials of their reliability on the ground? The fact that some of the Kerry brigades were barely operational less than four weeks after the visit would appear to substantiate this theory. From the Volunteers' point of view, with O'Donoghue gone, the pressure was off and they could afford to relax or relapse into the old way of doing things. Of course, particularly telling are statements made by the county's veterans to Ernie O'Malley in the late 1930s. These sidestep the standard folk interpretation and give a more complete picture of what was considered routine in Kerry when the conflict was at its height. 'It wasn't until 1921 that fellows did act on their own without any instructions from General Headquarters about attacking patrols or barracks,' said Michael Fleming, the adjutant with the Tralee Battalion up to the autumn of 1921. 'This shows that the area was very much behind hand.'[6] Every Volunteer was left 'to poke along for himself', agreed John Joe Rice of Tralee, but 'the organisation was then tightened up and you knew where you were'.[7]

Liam Lynch and other outsiders sent in to review the situation add to the picture of the Kerry rebels at this time. Lynch, in a three-page account sent to Headquarters in early October 1921, spoke of 'a complete lack of organisation in most battalion areas'. He described officers, particularly in the Kerry No. 1 Brigade area, as 'grossly' and 'completely incapable' of filling their positions and 'good fighting men' who had deteriorated into 'nothing more than undisciplined mobs' as a result of the inadequate leadership.[8] According to another report on the Kerry No. 1 Brigade written in June 1921, the entire battalion staff in Tralee, except for the quartermaster and the engineer, was considered 'bad' and 'too old and altogether too slow for the job'.[9] J.P. Kennedy, the intelligence officer in the town and a member of Paddy Cahill's brigade staff, was regarded as 'grossly incapable of filling the position'. 'His conduct in Tralee town in dealing with the enemy was nothing more than laughable', added Lynch, who saw little alternative but to request his immediate dismissal as an officer. He also advised that Michael Doyle, the battalion commandant, be removed since he was regularly absent and generally 'incapable' anyway owing to his 'advanced years'. Commandant Byrne, who was in charge of organisation within the brigade, was described as 'a complete failure', while Billy Mullins was considered 'entirely incapable'.[10]

'B' Company in Tralee town was described by Lynch as little more than a 'mob ... working in the wrong groove', with their captain himself described as 'a most unsatisfactory officer'. The commanding officers in Listowel and Ardfert, meanwhile, were 'sacked'.[11] They were also considered 'incapable', while Thomas Kennelly, an ex-RIC man and commandant of the Lixnaw Battalion, was 'to be got rid of at the first opportunity'. 'In a few words,' wrote Lynch, 'I never found it so humiliating to have to sit down and speak to such an officer. This area is simply a mob and will not be righted until officers are drawn from the ranks.'[12]

In all, IRA officials recommended the removal of nearly 50 per cent of the Kerry No. 1 brigade's officers.[13] However, as late as November 1921, Lynch was still complaining of a 'delay' on the part of GHQ to remove inefficient officers who were, in his opinion, mainly responsible for 'hampering' their efforts 'to make a brigade out of Kerry 1.'[14] 'Toleration of same at General Headquarters is partly responsible for non-development of this area for some months past,' complained Lynch in one particularly scathing report on the Kerry No. 1 Brigade, 'and if same does not cease I must give over the hope of getting this area into line in future'.[15]

Since local Volunteer units were more or less independent of any authority in Dublin, a strong case can be made against local brigade officers for failing to make better use of their battalions. It stands to reason that if the brigade staffs had been working and routinely checking the progress in each battalion, they would have picked up on the deteriorating situation on the ground. At least Paddy Cahill, O/C of the Kerry No. 1 Brigade, was in a position to inform Mulcahy in May 1921 that 'from a Volunteer point of view' things in his area 'could not (have been) much worse'.[16] However, as far as

Cahill was concerned, the fault lay not so much with him or his staff as with GHQ for failing to provide them with ammunition to carry on the fight effectively. 'Our activities have not been big,' he wrote, 'I explained that we had not the stuff to do much when in Dublin.'[17] Arguably, of course, this reflects poorly on Cahill. The consensus among Volunteers active at that time was that the input from GHQ only ever amounted to 'a little dribble of revolvers'; 'a few little pieces of stuff' at best.[18] If the men had any desire to fight it was up to them to find the guns to do so.[19] It did not reflect well on the fighting ability of a column if they were seen to be in any way dependent on outside support in order to operate.[20]

There are, however, indications that the men of Kerry No. 1 were not as badly off on the weapons front as Cahill seemed to think. In fact, there was 'a fair amount of arms' deposited in weapon stores around the brigade area.[21] An inspecting officer who visited the brigade in June 1921 found a situation where the commanding officers were out of touch with the situation on the ground. Battalions were seen 'working away independent of one another' without receiving assistance from either Cahill or any other member of the brigade staff.[22] Cahill 'plead(ed) guilty' only to leaving his correspondence unattended to: 'My reason being that I could go round to do a little work myself and see that the different battalion commandants carried on their work.'[23] Yet according to the officer's report the battalions of the Kerry No. 1 Brigade had for months been starved of 'a definite lead'. Cahill reportedly spent his time in a hut on the Dingle peninsula in command of a flying column which 'outside one or two operations had done nothing'.[24]

Dinny Daly, vice-commandant of the Cahirciveen battalion, gave an insight into rebel life under this leadership. The O/C

(Cahill) told them that they were 'not to take any action against the British for it had been planned to land arms in the Glen between Waterville and Ballinskelligs.'[25]

Liam Lynch later found the battalion in an abandoned state with all Volunteer activity having ceased in the area.[26] Was this on account of Cahill's order? By May, when there was still no effort made to land guns, Daly asked Richard Mulcahy about the instructions and the planned landing, and was told that 'there was no truth in it!'[27] It is possible that the order was simply the first step in another of what Bertie Scully called 'great plans' that never properly materialised.[28] If that was the case, then it was not so much the order as the absence of a countermanding one when it was decided not to go ahead with the plan.

Rebel activity in south Kerry was low-level anyway, even without orders against it from the leadership. This was due to the lie of the land. 'There was no real escape here,' stated Dinny Daly, 'for you were always in the open in this type of bare countryside.'[29] There were, however, 'very good lads' in Daly's battalion, and 'plenty' of them 'to help out'.[30] They had sufficient fighting potential and enough drive to make a go of their battalion. Yet, by April 1921, the fighting men had gone by the wayside and the Cahirciveen battalion was in crisis. There was 'complete inactivity'[31] in the area, 'bad communication' between the rebels and 'little or no organisation.'[32] How much of this was the fault of the leadership and the county's No. 1 Brigade? Reports from the area over the five-month period from February to June 1921 shows that Cahill's brigade leadership had little impact on the battalion; it is noteworthy that the level of rebel activity in Cahirciveen started to improve significantly in the weeks following Cahill's dismissal as commanding officer of the Kerry No.

1 Brigade.

Cahill was dismissed in late March 1921.[33] By mid-May rebel activity in the area had intensified to such an extent that enemy reinforcements had to be twice drafted in to contain the republican offensive.[34] According to one report:

> The road cutting and blocking had been so effective that the enemy was unable to rush his troops into the town and district of Cahirciveen. He was obliged to send them around by sea and then four days after being asked he has now to resort to bicycles for patrolling and this is confined to a radius of about two miles from town. Broken glass has been placed before such patrols, and from reports, with effect.[35]

In Waterville, meanwhile, the rebels were reportedly availing of every opportunity to enter the village 'with the intention of taking with small arms any straggling enemy'.[36] 'Men ambushing at different points during the day and some taking up positions during the night', confirmed the local IRA adjutant, 'but no opportunity of any kind has offered yet'. 'The police,' he added, 'are more or less confined to barracks since operations commenced in Cahirciveen.'[37] The situation became so bad from the authorities' point of view that by the end of May, M.J. O'Sullivan, a solicitor in Cahirciveen, was approached by the military in the area to act as mediator for them with the IRA. He was instructed to arrange possible terms for a ceasefire. 'This shows,' claimed one IRA officer, 'they have got too much of it and would like to be left alone in this out of the way area'[38]

'The enemy has now got more than he bargained for,' agreed Liam Lynch.[39] The reorganisation of the area into an independent brigade, which became known as the Kerry No. 3 Brigade, gave the south Kerrymen control over their own fortunes and gave them a better chance to show what they were really capable of. Incidences of officers holding the fighting men back did not just occur in the Kerry No. 1 Brigade area. In fact, Paddy Cahill's influence appeared from reports to be widespread. His influence extended into the Kerry No. 2 Brigade area and officers in the area were reluctant to act without first getting his approval.

Johnny Connors and Tom MacEllistrim, both active in the Kerry No. 2 Brigade, provided Ernie O'Malley with details of how their plans were frequently sabotaged by their own officers. When Connors of Farmers' Bridge requested his revolver from Joe Vale, the company captain, for an attack on a barracks at Field's Bridge, near Killarney, he was refused his weapon on the grounds that he 'was out of control in the area'. According to Connors, once he had informed Vale of plans to charge the barracks, word was sent to Paddy Cahill who immediately instructed that the project be abandoned. The men who had planned the operation learned shortly afterwards that information had been 'leaked' to the police from their own side so as to ensure that the attack would not take place. 'Cahill's excuse for all these acts was that you were spoiling a bigger thing – always he had that excuse,' stated Connors bitterly. The fact of the matter was that 'if you didn't do things with his authority he didn't like you to hold arms'.[40]

It was the usual practice, according to Connors, for the guns to be given to the officers 'for safe-keeping'. This method of doing things could, in fact, be seen to make sense especially at a time when weapons were scarce and the rebel 'defended (his) gun with (his) life' as distinct from the other way around.[41] This meant, however, that the officers in command had control of the bulk of the weapons and, crucially, made the decisions on how they should be used. Operationally speaking, this was not necessarily a bad thing as long as the officer was discerning enough to know the difference between a foolhardy assault and a more practicable one. In a situation where the officers lacked confidence it would, of course, have had a detrimental effect on the progress of a campaign.

Tom MacEllistrim had problems with the brigades' chief commandants when organising a second attack on Gortaclea Barracks and initially had to abandon his plans because of officers refusing to provide him with the necessary weapons. 'I went to Paddy Cahill in Tralee and I asked him for ammunition and he wouldn't do it,' recalled MacEllistrim. 'They refused (us) ammunition from Kerry 2 in Castleisland. Brigadier Dan O'Mahony, O/C Kerry 2 Brigade, also refused. Castleisland wouldn't give the ammunition unless it would be a success. I didn't know anyone in Dublin so I didn't know how to pull strings.'[42] A battalion could pay anything up to £50 for four rifles, so officers might have been reluctant to waste ammunition on an operation that they were not running themselves.[43] Nonetheless, the decision to refuse MacEllistrim is still surprising because of his standing; he was an experienced gunman with a solid track record. Besides, unless a fighting unit was encouraged to take some risks, it could not hope to build up its ammunition reserves, or the experience of its men for that matter.

Tom O'Connor, a commandant in Killorglin, though believing that they 'couldn't take the barracks' in the town, had enough confidence to go ahead with the attack, 'the idea (being) to give the men experience'.[44] Moreover, when Dan Allman's column increased its activity in the Kerry No. 2 area they captured 'thirty-two rifles and revolvers as men', while Johnny Connors, also active in east Kerry, noted that 'there was much more rifles' in his area when the IRA offensive was properly organised.[45] Increased action brought increased weaponry.

MacEllistrim managed eventually to get some ammunition from a rank-and-filer in Tralee for the attack at Gortaclea; interestingly, the man who supplied MacEllistrim had stolen his ammunition, more than 300 rounds, from an arms dump in his area.[46] MacEllistrim clearly was not the only rebel being deprived of ammunitions and other Volunteers also were going to extraordinary lengths to get ammunition to carry on the fight. The more serious fighters generally found some way of acquiring weapons and ammunition, and carried on the struggle using whatever they could get their hands on. The majority, however, took their lead from the officers in command, and the restraint exercised by them kept rebel activity in most areas to a minimum and prevented many good men from reaching their full potential as fighters.

'The Cahill influence', in particular, was described by IRA men across the county as a key factor in explaining the under-achievement of the Kerry rebels during the independence campaign. 'Everywhere I found that Cahill's influence was enormous,' wrote one IRA official to GHQ in June 1921. 'Whatever fault may have been found with his staff, the general and rooted conviction was that there was no man able to take his place and what made the situation worse no man was prepared to do so.'[47] Cahill, according to John Joe Sheehy, was 'a well up fellow who had been to college when few fellows got there'[48] and, in the light of Peter Hart's observations on the Cork IRA, was thus a 'natural choice for leader'.[49] 'He was a good man', stated Tom MacEllistrim, and, in the words of Dinny Daly, 'popular with the poorer classes in Tralee'. He 'was liked very much' and a proven patriot, having spent time in prison for his rebellious activities in 1916.[50]

Was this enough to account for the 'extraordinary hold'[51] Cahill had over the men? Johnny Connors was convinced that Cahill's influence was the result of calculated networking on his part, selecting the company captains himself, and playing it safe by sending out his own men to take up appointments in outlying battalions.[52] The manner in which Cahill came to have such a strong influence over the men was tied to their fortunes as rebels. The hesitancy of Cahill's officers in going against orders, and becoming actively involved in the fight, was a definite and important feature of the war in Kerry. 'We were very disciplined and told not to move without orders,' explained Michael Fleming, an adjutant with the Tralee Battalion.[53] This attitude, however, cost Fleming the confidence of his men 'owing to inactivity during hostilities' and he was later forced to resign his position.[54] Fleming's sense of duty was to Cahill first and foremost, and he was unwilling to go against orders and take matters into his own hands, even if it meant acting in the best interest of the men. He did not fail Cahill but the rank-and-file clearly felt that he failed them.

There were those in the county such as Connors and Tom MacEllistrim who 'did what they wanted' and 'ignored' Cahill 'for he wanted to court-martial them a couple of times'; even so, Ernie O'Malley heard enough from meeting with Kerry veterans to accept that Cahill was truly 'the important man' and 'it was he who got things going,'[55] Arguably, if Cahill had made more use of his position and adopted a more offensive approach, most of the county's battalions would have fallen in behind him. Instead, he had a tendency to wait for specific instructions from GHQ before contemplating any assault. This might explain why a number of the more dedicated fighters began to ignore brigade control and strike out on their own.

'General Headquarters wanted to make him fight more,' complained Dinny Daly, but 'Cahill was a shade careful. There had been a good many attempted ambushes, but nothing had come of them!'[56] 'It was Cahill who wanted instructions sent to him,' agreed Michael Fleming. 'We asked Cathal Brugha to give us a carte blanche with regard to ambushes, we wanted to disarm soldiers on the streets as they did in Fermoy and we came back with permission', but Cahill forbade it on the grounds that it was 'too daring'.[57] At the same time IRA reports show how officers were capable of jeopardising the success of an operation for a mere matter of protocol. Johnny Connors 'was brought over the coals' in August 1920 because he brought gunmen in from outside the battalion to assist with an ambush. 'I had Tom Mac and (Jack) Cronin with our company as they had experience,' explained Connors, but 'Paddy Cahill brought me over the coals after that (as to) why we should look for assistance from outside the area. Mac and Cronin just walked away. The lads got panicky and we (got) ready to withdraw.'[58]

Perhaps Cahill had good reasons for refusing to work with the Ballymacelligott men at this time. They were 'very unruly'[59] and, according to the men themselves, brought about their own transfer to the Castleisland Battalion in Kerry No. 2 by 'flouting' orders, 'ignoring' Cahill, and generally proving 'too hot for Kerry 1'.[60] Officers in Kerry, however, were as likely to be driven by their own egos as by national interest. County Kerry, according to one republican report in 1921, was something of 'a Mexico where cliques and factions abound(ed)' and intrusions of any kind were resented.[61]

Eamon Coogan, a local government official writing from the county in December 1921, provided some insight into this phenomenon when he wrote of the 'isolation' he had to endure among the 'wolves of Kerry'.[62] The arrival of 'the stranger', Andy Cooney, to the Kerry No. 1 area in April 1921 to replace Paddy Cahill as brigade O/C was received badly by the locals. 'He was no good,' stated Billy Mullins, 'he didn't get on with the lads!'[63] 'It caused a good deal of friction,' recalled Con Casey, 'a local man being succeeded by a fellow who came in from outside; naturally they were hostile to him. They had been together since before the Rising and most of them had seen action, been in jail or on hunger strike (together). They were loyal to the Brigadier Paddy Cahill and so were many others; Cooney could not make much heading here – he was in splendid isolation.'[64]

The men resented an outsider encroaching on their territory and usurping the role of their 'chief', but it did not necessarily take a complete stranger to get their backs up. John Joe Rice appears to have spent all his time 'tramping from one company to another fixing disputes and squabbles', while Denis Quill spoke at length of how 'local spite at work' in his area frequently resulted in 'tip top men' being overlooked for positions within the movement.[65] When 'Free' Murphy, the officer in command of Kerry No. 2, was transferred for a time from Castleisland to Kerry No. 1 pending the appointment of Cahill's successor, he was completely disregarded by the men and this despite the fact that he was from the county.[66] Local interests and factionalism were strong forces. The more 'clannish' rebels prided themselves on the belief that their battalions were 'the strongest' and their brigade 'the best in the division'.[67] Any suggestion that a unit was not up to standard, or of it being 'bested' by another faction, could cause serious resentment.

By mid 1921 the Kerry IRA, despite the in-house feuding, was beginning to find its feet. The Kerry No. 2 Brigade, in particular, earned the 'congratulations' of Richard Mulcahy, the Chief of Staff. He, incidentally, never imagined that 'the fighting material in the brigades (could have) promised to be so very fine'.[68] 'I hope that now Kerry 2 is definitely beginning to throw itself properly into the war', wrote Mulcahy after the IRA's success at Headford in March 1921, 'that no opportunity, however small, will be lost to show that Kerry 2 is not going to be behind any other brigade in the matter of initiative and in the matter of ability to strike a strong blow.'[69]

The emergence of a more confident Kerry No. 2 Brigade leadership, with Humphrey Murphy, Tom O'Connor and John Joe Rice in command, certainly improved fighting matters for a time and kept 'the Cahill influence' at bay. The British forces sensed a change in attitude and were worried by it. 'The IRA are practically all embodied,' wrote County Inspector O'Gerity in the summer of 1921, 'they scatter on the approach of a strong force and reassemble to commit outrage or to ambush a weak patrol.' 'In North Kerry flying columns roam about at a safe distance from police convoys and search parties', yet there were 'almost innumerable raids on stores, motor-cars, bicycles, post-offices, railway stations and cabins' reported, or an increase in those activities regarded as 'safe' for the rebels to engage in.[70]

From January to June 1921, the Kerry IRA limited its activity, on the whole, to the comparatively safe practices of raiding, road-trenching and mail robbery. Returns show, in fact, that despite a marked increase of almost 592 per cent in the number of outrages committed during this period, from 25 in January to 173 in June, only a fraction of these could be categorised as serious offences.[71] Out of a total of 225 outrages committed by rebels in April and May, for example, 188 (83 per cent) constituted the lesser offences of robbery, housebreaking, or assault, while murder and attempted murder accounted for just 16 per cent of all outrages. The figures for June were similar in that the less hazardous offences accounted for almost 90 per cent of all outrages that occurred with the remaining 10 per cent representing those of a more serious character.[72]

The small percentage in the number of serious outrages committed gives the impression that the Kerry rebels did not put themselves in the way of danger too often. The very increase in the number of offences shows, however, that neither were the fighting men of Kerry sitting on their laurels but instead were living up to O'Gerity's view of them as 'mobilised' and 'dangerous.'[73]

Furthermore, it seems fair to suggest that it was the presence of a handful of 'wandering gunmen' such as MacEllistrim, Allman Connors and Con Brosnan that made all the difference to the war. Their initiatives were singularly responsible for the triumphs at Headford, Clonbanin and Ballymacandy in 1921. If they had not defied the IRA leadership and engaged the British, the county could have been considerably lower down the activity scale than it proved to be.

That said, local IRA units had by the summer of 1920 done a good job of disabling the enemy administration in the county and, to their credit, of setting up a viable and working parish courts system. The republican court system was, according to one newspaper report in July, 'succeeding brilliantly in demonstrating its ability to administer justice'.[74] Sentences were given to 'good and lasting effect', was the view of one north Kerry commentator,[75] and 'the pity is', stated another, 'that the courts did not commence their operations earlier; the wanton destruction of much valuable property would have been prevented'.[76] The *Kerryman*, likewise, carried stories of Protestant litigants at republican courts, maintaining this was 'a striking example of the confidence in the power and justice' of the courts 'among all creeds and classes'.[77]

Moreover, reports to the IRA Adjutant-General indicated that the lesser men in the ranks were by no means idle, but busy burning unoccupied barracks, destroying income tax and customs records, while attempting to settle, in however unorthodox a manner, the land issue.[78] IRA activity was also considered widespread enough to include Kerry in the Martial Law Proclamation of December 1920. Despite this, the Kerry IRA remained some distance from becoming an effective guerrilla unit. That they had all the makings of one is a reasonable assumption owing to 'the good fighting spirit' that prevailed among the men, but they were ultimately held back by weak officers and poor leadership.

# 6

# LIKEABLE TANS AND UNLIKELY REBELS

Not all IRA officers in Kerry failed their men, and not all rank-and-filers doubted the courage and abilities of the officers leading them. Paddy Cahill undoubtedly had supporters, and he was generally considered by his fellow commandants to be 'the most efficient officer to fill the post of brigade O/C'. In fact, his dismissal was against the expressed wishes of all the battalion officers in the Kerry No. 1 Brigade area.[1] To them the accusations were unjust. So how did they explain the limited activity of the Kerry rebels at this time?

In a letter to Richard Mulcahy in May 1921, shortly after his dismissal, Cahill made a significant point in his defence. He commented on the 'terrible alarm' British reprisal action had caused throughout his area.[2] While outlining the difficulties he and his staff faced in attempting to 're-organise' the men in the weeks immediately following enemy reprisals, Cahill touched on a factor not often admitted to in the folklore of the period: the fighting men of County Kerry suffered from their nerves. It was fear and inexperience that held them back, not overcautious officers. This raises questions about the robustness of the county's IRA men and whether they really were the born fighters that they are depicted as in nationalist histories and popular traditions.

There were those in the county, stated one south Kerry officer, 'known to lose the head once the firing started'.[3] 'The men got panicky,' admitted Johnny Connors; indeed, he recalled how his unit had to withdraw from an ideal ambush position on the Tralee-Killorglin road in August 1920 because of consternation among the fighting men. Billy Mullins, likewise, had his own troubles at Ballymacandy when the Keel men 'got sick during the fight' and had to 'lie down' until the shooting stopped.[4] It was only 'when the strain came on we knew who was who', said Tom Daly, who was active with the Kerry No. 2 Brigade.[5] His remarks indicate that the county's rebels, though spirited enough 'when things were quiet', were not as willing to volunteer for active service once the conflict became violent.[6]

Police reports from the period confirm this as fact. It is clear from the records that the level of IRA activity began to diminish from late-summer 1920 as the British counter-offensive gained momentum. Reinforcements were drafted into the county from early June and among them were Black-and-Tans and Auxiliary-type forces.[7] The arrival of the new recruits did not worry the rebels initially and the republican 'terrorism' continued throughout June and July.[8] It took some time, and not a little action, to convince the county's rebels of the newcomers' true propensity for violence. The tables had turned by mid-winter 1920. As Crown Forces' activity reached an unprecedented high with the November 'terror' (a direct result of an IRA 'outbreak' in late October following Terence MacSwiney's death) the rate of rebel activity slowed. IRA outrages committed in the county fell from 75 in October 1920 to 25 in January 1921.[9]

In December 1917, RIC County Inspector, G.M. Heard, attributed a 'dying out of enthusiasm' for Sinn Féin activity to 'the season of Christmas'. 'As a rule,' he wrote, 'men are careful (not) to do anything that would risk their arrest and confinement at Christmas time and for a few weeks before Christmas shop assistants and indeed farmers are kept very busy.'[10] Was Christmas also a factor in slowing IRA activity in late 1920? The fact that the number of outrages increased again in February 1921 to 56, and continued to increase on average by approximately 53 per cent each month afterwards, suggests that the time of year played a part.[11] Add this factor to the 'violence of reprisals undertaken' by the Crown Forces during November 1920 and it is little wonder that IRA fighters decided to lie low for a while.[12] However, it is clear that the RIC were convinced there was more to it than this. 'There seems to be some little sign,' wrote the County Inspector in October 1920, 'that the murder gang is finding it more difficult to draw the whole body with them in their schemes.'[13] 'The number of those willing to engage in this sort of work is believed to have fallen off,' he reported, and 'the police have reason to believe that efforts are being made to force young men into this body to enable these murderous enterprises to continue.'[14]

Police reports, however, show that there were already in excess of 3,000 men in the movement.[15] Why would the Kerry IRA be 'conscripting' new blood into their ranks when they had an ample rank-and-file available? Perhaps, the IRA men involved in outrage thought better of it when 'things got rough' and the stakes were raised.[16] The murders of John Leen and Moss Reidy at Ballymacelligott on Christmas night by the Crown Forces brought home to a lot of the men the kind of risks they were taking. Was the Republic worth one's life? This reminds us of Tom Daly's remarks about real strain separating the men from the boys; violent enemy action was halting IRA activity. With the county's rebels starting to give 'bail for their good behaviour', the Kerry IRA might well have had to take action and start conscripting a new membership.[17]

When one considers the nature of the British campaign, it is not difficult to appreciate why some of the county's IRA men might have become, as one RIC district inspector observed, 'more reluctant to engage in outrage'.[18] There appears, on the whole, to be very little in the way of evidence that contradicts the traditional view that the 'depraved' Black-and-Tans, and the Auxiliary forces dispatched to Ireland during that summer of 1920 were anything other than 'the scum of the earth'.[19] They were, in Cardinal Logue's estimation, little more than 'a horde of savages'. 'Some of them, if not many', he accused, '(were) simply brigands, burglars and thieves'. They were 'Huns', maintained another, whose 'instances of attack made revolting reading'.[20] 'Their methods were certainly not of the kid-glove and rose water variety,' agreed C.H. Bretherton.[21] Peig Sayers from west Kerry likewise remarked, 'You'd think it was down in the bowels of a ship they had spent their lives.'[22] They were described as a 'mob'[23] by Sayers; were 'savage forces let loose',[24] according to Fr James O'Sullivan of Abbeydorney; and in the view of Ballydonoghue man Densie Collins were 'a wild kind of an organisation'.[25]

The British Labour Party Commission, sent to Ireland in November 1920 to investigate claims of atrocity by the British armed forces, recounted how with 'feelings of shame' they witnessed for themselves the 'insolent swagger' of the Tan; they were 'rough', 'brutal', 'abusive' and 'distinctly the worse for liquor'.[26] 'None of them looked like men', recalled Mrs A.E. Robinson, an Englishwoman and member of the Women's International League, when called before the American Commission in December 1920. 'They were all wild drunk', stated another, and depicted in many contemporary accounts as 'burglars', 'highway robbers', 'gunmen' and 'petty thieves' with a 'ruthlessness and all-pervading character without parallel'.[27] Brigadier-General F.P. Crozier, who resigned as commander of the Auxiliaries in late November 1920, spoke of 'the most appalling orgy of bloodletting and lust' by 'selected and foul men for a grossly foul purpose'. 'Never before,' he cried, 'has the King's RIC been used to murder, rob, loot, and burn up the innocent because they could not catch the few guilty on the run.'[28]

Most Kerry republicans agreed that the Tans 'blackguarded it' in the county.[29] Some, however, did argue that the auxiliary forces were a 'mixed lot physically and mentally'.[30] Dingle, by all accounts, had its share of 'ruffians' and 'dangerous terrorists', but there were also 'not a few who seemed decent enough'.[31] Con Casey wrote of the Black-and-Tans that he encountered in the County Jail in Tralee while he was there:

> One was gentle, as gentle a young man as ever I met. A most unlikely Black and Tan. He told me that after being demobbed from the army and when there was no work to be got in England and he had a mother and sisters to support he joined the Black and Tans. He was certainly anything than a Black and Tan in manner and outlook. The other was a rough spoken, foul-mouthed Scotsman, called, as you might expect, Jock. He was fluent in bad language and he wrote it on the cell walls, faded white, with the point of a 303 bullet.[32]

'Some of the Black and Tans were all right', was the view of one ex-Constable named Dunne, who was stationed in Kenmare:

> Some of them were decent fellows, (but) some of them were a real damned nuisance especially when they got drink taken; Some weren't fit nor even accustomed to policing, but, you know, there were some fine fellows among them.[33]

Christy O'Grady spoke of the 'great spirit of friendliness' that was seen to exist in Killorglin between the people and the Tans.[34] 'The Tans in Killorglin were not bad to prisoners', according to Bertie Scully, while the same was said by Dinny Daly of the military in Cahirciveen, who, apart from occupying houses in the town, 'never had a permanent garrison there'.[35] However, the republicans never left their guard down when it came to the Tans. They were not to be trusted. Con Casey could find himself chatting easily to an injured Tan while on cleaning duty and even get a snap of him for his family album but was still aware that an IRA prisoner was 'being beaten up' upstairs: 'That produced an atmosphere of apprehension as it could be the treatment that others of us could expect.'[36]

The moral conduct of the Auxiliary forces, and the Tans in particular, was not consistent with that of the regular troops. They were capable of acts, which the American Commission described as 'contrary to all law and all standards of human practice'. Their conduct left so much to be desired in Kerry that the county's soldiers, even at the higher levels of command, were either informing against the Auxiliaries or deserting 'in disgust'.[37] Billy Mullins described how Captain O'Malley, in particular, 'always passed on word to (them) about the doings of the Tans, of their threats and their intentions to shoot-up places and he sent in complaints about their alleged activities'.[38]

Mullins also referred to a Captain Townsend in the town 'who was very decent', but it was Colonel Berkerly, the officer in command of the East Lancashire Regiment in Tralee, that stuck out in Tadg Kennedy's memory since he was well known to have 'hated the Auxies and the Tans'. 'We got our information from friendly RIC who were with them acting as guides,' claimed Kennedy. 'Practically all the RIC with a few exceptions were on our side.'[39]

Kennedy's view of a sympathetic RIC force was not universally held. A report on RIC attitudes towards the IRA taken in eight barracks in the Kerry No. 2 area showed that the police were mainly unsympathetic. The report, compiled by the IRA and dated November 1921, shows in fact that more than three-quarters of the constables in six of the barracks mentioned were hostile. Of the seventeen constables in the Killarney barracks, for example, nearly all were regarded as hostile including one constable named Long, described as a 'religious maniac'. The same was said of the barracks at Kenmare, Rathmore, Brosna and Killorglin. At Cahirciveen, in the Kerry No. 3 area, of the 28 constables stationed in the district, 'all were hostile' with the exception of Constables Whelan and Daly, Sergeant Heavey and Head Constable Hopkins who were classed as 'indifferent'. In total, out of 105 constables mentioned in the report, 84 (or more than 80 per cent) were considered definitely hostile, while a further ten were regarded as 'neutral', 'inoffensive' or 'non-aggressive'. Only eight were believed to be 'friendly' or at least 'not hostile.'[40]

IRA views on the RIC were not clear cut, and opinions varied across the county. Tadg Kennedy's view was favourable and he referred to men like Jimmy Duffy, the county inspector, as 'an old schoolmate of mine and Paddy Cahill's' and therefore friendly. Dan Mulvihill did not agree: 'The RIC were always looking for someone to kick about.' 'They had been for so long Cock of the Walk, they couldn't conform!'[41] Denis Quill reckoned, 'we didn't handle them properly for their brothers were in the IRA.' John Joe Rice, active in Kerry No. 2, was of the opinion that while 'no one' from the RIC seemed inclined to provide the rebels with information, neither would they 'identify wanted men' for the British.[42]

When it came to discussing the conduct of the Tans (who were officially part of the RIC), IRA testimony was less understanding. 'They raided continuously,' claimed Billy Mullins. 'Shot up the towns' said Tom MacEllistrim, and in Con Casey's opinion they typically 'kicked the stuffing' out of the men they rounded up.[43] Christy O'Grady wrote of 'drunken Tans' smashing in houses 'looking for drink', the 'great fear of reprisals', and of police out 'in civies firing shots' and 'beating chaps down the street'.[44] 'They glory in all their raiding, flogging and shooting', mourned one anonymous observer from Newtownsandes in May 1921. 'The language they use is abominable', cried Mary Dowling, a young nurse home on leave in August 1920, and according to Fr O'Donoghue of Ballymacelligott, their conduct was 'inexcusable'.[45]

'To pretend that there is no general police terror (here) is sheer hypocrisy,' wrote *Daily News* journalist Hugh Martin in a report from the county in late October 1920. In retaliation for the IRA cropping of one girl's hair, 'they cropped the hair of four others, beat six young men with the stocks of their rifles till they were black and blue, burnt several ricks and set a creamery on fire doing damage to the extent of from £10,000 to £12,000'. They took one young man named Maurice Lovett into 'the pelting rain in his night-shirt' and 'in the presence of his mother they beat him with their rifles, knocked him down and kicked him where he lay in the mud'.[46] In

Tralee, a group of Irish Volunteers was attacked by Black-and-Tans as they were returning from a picture theatre. The Tans used trench tools on them. At Ballymacelligott, according to Hugh Martin's inquiries, two brothers were taken out in their shirts and bare feet 'and made to stand with their faces to the wall and their hands above their heads at either end of the cottage where they were clubbed'.[47]

Moss Horgan, who was involved with the IRA in Tralee, was, in Johnny Connors' view, 'in a devil of a way for a long time as a result of the battering he got' from being tied to a colt's legs and dragged along a road by Major John MacKinnon. MacKinnon was the commander of the Auxiliary forces in the town.[48] Denis Quill described how he was 'beaten up' by two Auxiliary officers, 'one a captain, the other a colonel', while Tomas Ó Clumhain, in a report to IRA GHQ in May 1921, gave details of the 'very brutal treatment' he received at the hands of the police at O'Dorney. It was, he explained, 'really savage. I was taken out four times and beaten with a rifle – (Sergeants) Restrick and Lalor being particularly savage.'[49] Meanwhile, Con Dee, the only survivor of the 'massacre' at Gortaglanna in May 1921, described in his statement how he and three other Irish Volunteers were treated by the Tans before they were executed. They were forced to undress and 'while fastening (their) clothes again were beaten with rifles, struck with revolvers and thrown on the ground and kicked in trying to save (themselves).' He continued:

> Four or five men came round each of us and my captors continued to beat me with their rifles and hit me with their fists ... I saw blood on Jerry Lyons' face and on Paddy Walsh's mouth. Paddy Dalton was bleeding from the nose. We were then asked to run but we refused. We were again beaten with the rifles and ordered into a field by the roadside. We asked for a trial but the

*Likeable Tans and Unlikely Rebels*

Black and Tans laughed and jeered and called us murderers.[50]

Lady Albinia Broderick, who was in Tralee town when the bodies were brought back to the barracks, wrote of the incident to a friend:

> They must still have been, or one of them must have been alive for the blood was still running from the lorry when it came in. They were left for two hours in the barrack yard, by which time they were already dead. The face of one, a fine young fellow whom I knew personally, was all smashed in.[51]

'It wasn't the first organised job of the kind by the heads of the forces in charge,' claimed another.[52] In fact, Reverend J.J. O'Sullivan of Killeentierna, a parish on the outskirts of Killarney, gave details of a similar outrage perpetrated by the Tans against John O'Connor, 'a poor small farmer', arrested outside a Sinn Féin court in the area in December 1920. 'He never was one way or the other connected with the IRA', claimed the priest, but 'he was arrested, put into the lorry and kept in the lorry all day long'. When the Tans had finished with him the neighbours found him,

> (L)ying in the road with bullet wounds all through him. Legs, thighs smashed in, hands broken, things of that kind and his account was they beat him in the lorry and then threw him out on the road and fired a number of shots at him. I saw myself, his thigh bone out through his trousers and his hands broken out, then thrown out on the road as the lorry was moving and shot.[53]

When the Tans returned by the same route some hours later and learned that O'Connor was still alive, they sought him out and 'fired three shots into his skull'.

There was one wound through the cheek and I saw the bullet marks in the wall behind his head. He lived for four hours afterwards breathing, yet unconscious.[54]

The accounts of Black-and-Tan and Auxiliary brutality are wide-ranging and come from a large cross-section of the Kerry community. They are sufficient in themselves to accuse the Tans and Auxiliary forces with gross misconduct during this period. The fact that 'combat was being carried out on foul lines',[55] as General Crozier put it, also provides an explanation as to why some republicans might have taken the decision to abandon the fight and reconsider their positions within the IRA.

The IRA man had to think about the consequences for his family. A rebel's family was targeted by the Tans for reprisal actions and was generally in danger if the activist was a wanted man. May Dálaigh, sister of Tom and Charlie Daly, recalled how their family home was burned down by the Tans as a reprisal for the shooting of two officers in Castleisland in May 1921. 'We had not a stick of furniture (left)', she related to Uinseann MacEoin, 'everything was consumed.'[56] Reverend J.J. O'Sullivan, in a statement to the military in early 1921, explained how another young man named Murphy 'would have been shot' had he not left home once his brother went on the run:

His father's house was set on fire and burned to the ground. The neighbours told me it is simply nonsense expecting that young Murphy would come here because he would never get home alive.[57]

Fears for their own safety, and that of their families hampered the IRA fight in Kerry. Moreover, Volunteers were afraid already

*Likeable Tans and Unlikely Rebels*

because of their inexperience as fighters. With little experience, and almost no access to weapons, the men did not have the means or the confidence to go out and create the opportunities to fight. Con Brosnan, active with the north Kerry flying column, hinted that even when the guns were made available for an assault, as was the case in January 1921 when plans were being finalised for the shooting of Sergeant O'Sullivan in Listowel, the men could be slow to volunteer. This was not surprising with only obsolete weapons available and little in the way of experience or training.[58]

Just days before the Truce came into effect in July 1921, officers in the Kerry No. 2 Brigade area were still found to be attributing casualties within their ranks to the fact that some of the men had never before been under fire.[59] There was 'no systematic training' in evidence in the Kerry No. 1 Brigade and hardly 10 per cent of the men were able to use a rifle.[60] Moreover, the report indicates that the distribution of guns to the battalion areas was not consistently done in relation to the number of men active on the rolls or ammunition available. Out of seven companies in the Ardfert battalion, for example, four had well over the quota required for the number of men active, yet in Ballyheigue, where there was over 100 'reliable' men, twelve shotguns were all that was to be had between them. Fifty or so rebels at Keel, in the Killorglin battalion, had to battle it out amongst themselves for the ten shotguns in the company stores, unlike Glenbeigh, in the same battalion, where twenty men held at least 30 sound weapons and over 250 rounds of ammunition. Just a handful of men in B Company, Killorglin, controlled fifteen rifles, twenty shotguns and almost 300 rounds of ammunition. This was also the case in Farmers' Bridge, in the Tralee Battalion, where 30 fighting men had responsibility for twenty shotguns, any number of service rifles, and three Mills bombs in its munitions store. The twelve men left behind in the Listowel Company had rifles, shotguns and 40 sticks of gelignite; all this while the 200 or so 'promising' Volunteers in the Dingle area were unable to operate effectively 'owing to the great want of arms' that existed in their area.[61] It must also be considered that just because a battalion looked to have a considerable weapons hold, many of the guns were often rendered useless, having been destroyed by dampness after being hidden outside or by not having the correct ammunition supplied.

According to Cork IRA officer Liam Deasy, the disproportion was often caused by an 'enthusiasm' on the part of his county's brigade staff to boost the activities of weaker battalions by transferring ammunition to inactive areas.[62] The relative wealth of a battalion area might also have had a bearing on the amount of weapons it had. The difference in the quantity of ammunition held, for example, by the west Kerry battalions and those around Listowel, a prosperous agricultural district in the north of the county, might be explained in terms of money. In Dingle it was reported that 'living conditions were wretched' and 'the state of impoverishment' that existed was not 'wholly attributable' to the Black-and-Tans.[63] A lack of money by battalions in the area could be cited as a factor in explaining how the 280-strong Volunteer corps had access to only 22 shotguns, nine revolvers and twelve rifles, three of which were out of order. This represented less than half of the total amount of arms used by the 30 or so 'reliables' in Newtownsandes, a single company in the comparatively more prosperous Listowel battalion area.[64]

By all appearances, the Dingle battalion had its share of problems. Liam Lynch was of the opinion that Commandant Moriarty, the battalion chief, did not measure up at all but was 'entirely incapable' and was the main reason why the Black-and-Tans had 'such a shocking free hand' in the Dingle area. It was the view of officials that republican activity in the Dingle area during 1920-21 was 'far worse than in pre-war days' as a result of those left in charge.[65]

IRA reports showed in general, however, that brigade officers in the county were decidedly indifferent when it came to the running of the division, with weapons being 'badly distributed with regard to suitability of ammunition' and the brigade quartermaster unable even to provide GHQ with a list of arms held.[66] It has already been shown that the area's officers were not all that forthcoming with weapons, but it would also seem that even when weapons were provided, IRA activists could find themselves without the correct ammunition. Con Brosnan and the north Kerry flying column had to rely on borrowed rifles from the Tarbert company for the attack on Sergeant O'Sullivan in January 1921. At least they could be sure they had ammunition for them and the weapons were in good working order.[67]

The IRA in Kerry feared the Black-and-Tans, but the more active rebels in the county never cited them as a reason for not fighting. In their view the lack of fighting was down to a shortage of weapons, bad distribution of ammunition and limited experience. In Tom Barry's experience also, 'there was little enthusiasm' in west Cork, except from some 30 or so hardliners, 'to seek a second term in the Flying Column service in their own area'. The risks were too great even in Barry's region which was generally considered to be one of the most active areas in the country.[68] Lack of ammunition or experience never hindered the more hard-line rebels, but it certainly affected the ordinary rank and filer in seriously committing to the fight.

# 7

# WAR IN PEACE: A BATTLE OF WILLS

From the first there had been bickering and jealousies, and clan feuds and secret society intrigues in the Sinn Féin ranks, but while the fight was still on the priests and the women managed to keep the disputants from turning their backs on the common enemy to engage in the more congenial task of chewing the ears off one another. It was inevitable that once the Truce came and there were no more Crown Forces to do in and be done in by, domestic quarrels would be the order of the Sinn Féin day.
(C.H. Bretherton, 1925).[1]

Con Casey, contrary to the image held by C.H. Bretherton, remembered that summer of 1921 when the Truce came as 'a glorious summer of long sunny days'.[2] 'There was a feeling of intense relief,' he declared. 'A great feeling of euphoria', recalled John Joe Sheehy.[3] According to Pádraig Long of Dingle, it was 'a prolonged holiday' when 'Volunteers could return to their homes' and 'beautiful blue skies shone down on the equally blue waters of the harbour and the bay.'[4] 'People were elated', wrote one reporter from Tralee town.[5] 'As if from tension,' continued Casey, '(they) came into the streets and began to walk around Ballyard and along the Canal Bank.'[6] 'What a change!' declared Christy O'Grady:

> Myles sold a ticket (Aid IRA) to Gussy the Tan. (They) take the abuse they get in very good part. Great crowd in the shop – some wanted men in town. Saw Mick Leary and most of the lads. It's almost like old times now![7]

It certainly was a good summer to be a young man if O'Grady's diary is anything to go by and more so if you were a young man with IRA connections. Those 'war-worn troops' were, in the words of one Kerry No. 2 officer, 'now on a holiday'.[8] They had earned the right to 'stay in bed unaccountably', 'dance all night' and spend their time 'fooling' or 'playing cards'.[9]

There were also people in John Joe Sheehy's view who had never been active 'trying to take advantage of things'.[10] The Truce saw self-regarding 'heroes' and 'trench-coat' types emerge from the woodwork. In the area to the west of Dingle, the average number on parade increased by almost 450 per cent (from 182 in June 1921 to 1,000 in September). This figure was practically double that of the entire strength of the Dingle battalion before the Truce and over five times the number of those considered reliable.[11] The Ballymacelligott company, likewise, had only about 70 men within its ranks during the war and 'never more than 40 for active service', but by early September 1921 there were reports of 700 Volunteers and upwards on parade.[12] Companies in the area had joined with the Ballymacelligott Volunteers for the visit of Tom Barry and this might account for the huge increase, though the figure was, by any standards, still remarkable for a company that up to that point had never more than 150 Volunteers on parade. Similarly, the Killarney battalion was reported to have had a turnout that ran 'into some five or six thousand men' on one day in September 1921.[13] This figure was practically double the number of enrolled Volunteers for the entire Kerry No. 2 Brigade area. According to official IRA sources, the Volunteers in the No.2 area amounted to just 3,398 men, including officers, in August 1921.[14] Jeremiah Murphy also described huge turnouts throughout the rest of this area. 600 east Kerrymen were out on parade in Gneevegullia 'on a warm Saturday in September',[15] with further reports of 'about a thousand men' on manoeuvre in Glenflesk in October when just three Battalions, Kenmare, Killarney and Rathmore, congregated for inspection.[16]

Significant outside interest in the Volunteers was short-lived and really only in evidence in the six weeks or so after the Truce. Reports show, in fact, that men who in July 1921 'crowded' onto the roof of a train so as not to be left out of an excursion to Fenit were, by mid-September, refusing to attend IRA practice.[17] 'Pretty exciting evening,' wrote Christy O'Grady on 10 September 1921. 'Very few attended. (There were) five of us and the officer sent us to round them up. Had to drag a few. One drew a jack-knife. After hard work (we) gathered most of them. They made one attempt en masse to get away but failed. Court-martials for five as a result.' By early January 1922 there were more absent and it was, according to O'Grady, much 'tougher' to get the men together.[18]

Numbers on parade by November had begun to resemble the turnouts reported for June, indicating that the majority of those who appeared at the time of the Truce were probably hanger-on types that lost interest in the movement as soon as the celebrations died down.[19] The 'trucileer' type was often and conveniently blamed for crimes that took place against communities during the ceasefire. To be fair, the evidence has shown that the county's rebels could be just as culpable. *An t-Óglach*, the IRA paper, commented that in an atmosphere where rebels were applauded or, as they put it, 'hero-worshipped' and 'subjected on all sides to influences and temptation", IRA abuse of its position was always in danger of becoming more commonplace.[20]

'Men that had been great men, that never drank before, people made much of them,' reckoned May Dalaigh, and 'they got swelled heads.'[21] John Joe Sheehy agreed:

Some of the fellows who had been out on the run, who had been strong in the Movement, lost their heads too much. It was a difficult period; the toughest six months I ever had, administering a county in a country that was slowly slipping into Civil War.[22]

Sheep, cattle, land, even hotels were all commandeered 'in the name of the IRA' at that time.[23] There was justification for some seizures, as in Cahirciveen when the IRA confiscated a Ford car valued at £250 belonging to local publican Julia Guerin; her brother had evaded payment of a fine to the Sinn Féin court on foot of some indiscretion or other with a servant girl in the family's care.

In a lot of other cases, however, reports show that IRA violations were for the most part unwarranted. Consider Ellen O'Leary of Castlecove, Cahirciveen, who was shot at and forced out of the hotel she managed when she refused admittance to a party of 60 armed men who wanted it as a barrack; or the dilemma of Colonel Warden in Kenmare, who by 19 October 1921 had been raided by the IRA as many as nineteen times since the start of the Truce. A man called O'Shea from Glenbeigh likewise blamed rebels for taking the bull and yearling heifer that went missing from his land in early October.[24] O'Shea was not the first farmer in this area to have had animals seized in this manner. Moreover, the time of year and the fact that the thieves took the trouble to select good breeding stock raises doubts about whether the animals were intended, as was the story, to provide for men at a training camp. The Truce afforded many of the fighting men, 'fed up with soldiering',[25] with an opportunity to settle down and it is possible that O'Shea's animals were taken by an IRA man for farming purposes.

White Cross money[26] was especially useful in setting a fellow up for life and was distributed more readily among members of the IRA after the Truce.[27] Tadg Kennedy, an IRA man and accountant with the County Council, appealed to 'the White Cross people' to advance £600 to the Ardfert battalion commandant, a draper by profession, so that he could buy a house and set up a business.[28] Perhaps it was the prospect of peace that prompted many in White Cross circles to adopt a more relaxed approach and make the society's funds more widely available to the IRA and their dependants.[29] Whatever the motives involved, rebel activity would seem to show that a proverbial free-for-all existed in the county in the wake of the ceasefire with men 'boasting about what they would do when they got home rule'.[30]

'It is very plain,' wrote the IRA Chief of Police in August 1921, 'that quite a number of men, and in some cases officers, are indulging in excesses which do not tend to maintain the good name of the Army.' On the other hand, the chief understood 'the natural tendency' on the part of the men who had been fighting 'to enjoy themselves during the Truce'.[31] He was not going to become overly concerned by reports that members of the IRA were 'generally guilty of acts which (were) offensive against the civil code'.[32] In fact he continued to adopt an open-minded approach in relation to the men.

In any case, IRA reports showed that by November 1921 the Kerry No. 2 and Kerry No. 3 brigade areas were generally considered 'well-controlled' with the officers in command believed to be 'working their departments well' and 'availing fully of (all) possibilities', however limited, in their areas.[33] Indeed, even as early as August, when communications to GHQ were admitting that IRA members were 'the chief offenders in frequenting public houses after hours' and were 'fraternising and drinking with Enemy Police', reports still showed significant improvement in the divisions. Kerry No. 2, in particular, was reported to have 'developed enormously'.[34] 'The best results were being obtained' in most areas, according to an IRA report in November, and local officers were, for once, up to speed and in position to act if the men got too out of hand.[35]

However, Kerry No. 1 was proving to be the fly in the ointment, as the men were no longer complying with orders from acting officers. Abuses remained widespread and the 'discredit' to which the army had been brought there was, in the view of one local officer writing in mid-October, of 'a far more serious type than in Cork No. 3.'[36] Officers were 'working against all odds' to restore order in an area which, the same report alleged, had become 'four times harder to run since the Truce.'[37] It was an area that had always presented difficulties, and it is difficult to understand why GHQ was unable to anticipate some level of resistance to the 'sweeping changes' introduced to the local leadership in the early summer of 1921. At the very least, it showed a serious lack of foresight. 'It certainly was an upheaval', recalled Con Casey, and regarded by some as:

> (S)omething akin to a take-over by the Young Turks; John Joe Sheehy took the brunt of it in Tralee and I came in for a good share of it. As adjutant I was young by the standards of the men I was dealing with and possibly regarded by some of them as an upstart. I had to take an active part in prosecuting some of them and questioning them on their lack of aggression in their areas before the Truce; there are few now who remember or have heard of that forgotten feud. Those who were actively engaged in it, the brigade staff, the battalion O/Cs who were displaced and those who succeeded them are all dead. The friction generated was bitter and long-lived, especially in Tralee, where men who knew each other for years took sides and became definitely unfriendly. Some of us would pass each other on the street for years without the customary acknowledgement or salutation.[38]

Liam Lynch had always been of the opinion that Paddy Cahill, though unproductive, should be left in position and an efficient staff elected instead. GHQ, however, decided to take action and removed him. Reports had shown that Cahill was incapable of properly utilising any staff and, GHQ could not allow the fighting units in Kerry to continue to exist 'in name only'.[39]

That said, in terms of the damage caused to relations between the county's IRA men and GHQ later on, the gamble might not have been worth the risk. Visiting officials were given fair warning of the extent of Cahill's support in the area and, judging by one source, this support was extensive enough to suggest that Cahill was 'the only man' able 'to hold the Brigade together'.[40] Tadg Brosnan, the officer in command of the 4th Battalion at Castlegregory, though under orders, refused to accept the vacant position and 'no amount of argument could induce him to do so', explained one official in June. He continued:

> His nominal reason was unfitness for the post but it was palpable that he was acting from a feeling of loyalty to Cahill. Under these circumstances, I decided not to approach any other officer as I was sure I would be turned down; if I proceeded with Officers in turn I would ultimately have (had) to suspend every Officer in the Brigade.[41]

However, despite such reports, GHQ persisted in believing that the removal of Paddy Cahill was essential. It is remarkable that the hostile reaction did not lead them to understand that having a brigade that was only partly active could still prove more advantageous in the long run than one that refused categorically to carry out any orders. This is not to say that there were not definite improvements made in the organisation of the area as a whole once Cahill was removed. Nevertheless, if GHQ had gone for the lesser of the two evils and reconsidered Cahill's position as leader, they would have stood more of a chance of getting the brigade back in tow and, crucially, of lessening the likelihood of a split emerging later on. What good were capable new commandants if the men were refusing to even acknowledge them, let alone take orders from them?

John Joe Sheehy, the man who famously shot the 'brazen' Major

McKinnon in April 1921, was criticised by many when he stepped up to take command in Tralee, despite the fact that he was the 'obvious choice' for the position. B Company, based at Strand Street, 'did not co-operate with him,' wrote Con Casey, 'believing then and for years afterwards that he was active in the demotion of Paddy Cahill to whom B Company were devoted.' Tadg Brosnan, meanwhile, refused to recognise the new Brigadier, Andy Cooney, 'and let it be known that his Brigade O/C was Paddy Cahill.'[42] Bertie Scully also seemed set against anyone other than Cahill acting as leader, insisting that when 'Free' Murphy took over the brigade, 'there was no activity until the order the night before the Truce to attack all barracks'. 'I had an empty feeling about it', he stated, when questioned about Cahill's suspension. 'We demanded reasons' and 'Liam Lynch got red in the face and said it was an order. Then I wrote out my resignation as Vice O/C but Mulcahy said resignations would not be accepted.'[43]

The officials who lobbied for reorganisation in the weeks before the Truce apparently believed that 'a better spirit and understanding' would result once the men noticed 'a change', and indeed the work of the brigade was seen to improve.[44] The same could not be said of the men at GHQ in October 1921, who, despite continuous reports of 'trouble' in the area and 'great uneasiness amongst the best men in the brigade' owing to the delay 'in fixing up the Paddy Cahill business', still refused to back down on decisions made months earlier, thought the situation had deteriorated, and that there was every possibility of the brigade 'suffering grievously' as a result.[45]

Though GHQ was trying hard for the first time in the war to impress its authority on the men outside Dublin, the attitude in Kerry was still unforgiving. The Kerrymen were certainly 'sick and tired of the trouble', but they had no intention of bowing to anything that would 'make it appear that they were beaten on their point', even though, as Humphrey Murphy, the new acting commandant of Kerry No. 1,[46] plainly pointed out, 'the question of Cahill (did) not now arise at all as far as the O/Cs were concerned.'[47] The fact that the new men appointed were 'as a majority prepared to carry on irrespective of who the Brigade officers were'[48] should have been surety enough for GHQ to realise that the brigade would eventually come through. It was certainly a good opportunity for them to diffuse tensions by giving the men what they wanted and reappointing Cahill as Staff Officer. Whether Cahill would have accepted the position is entirely a different matter, but at least GHQ would have been seen to make good their 'serious lapse in judgement' and this might have earned them an extra measure of support in the run up to the vote on the Treaty.

There was more to the 1922 split than the Republic. Rebels who 'had lost little sleep over the winning of it' in the first place were not about to become patriots overnight.[49] The young men of Keel, for instance, had no qualms about compromising their principles for the promise of 'so many thousand pounds for work',[50] while in Killarney the IRA who went Free State did so more for 'the job and plenty to eat' than anything else.[51] 'They were not particularly enthusiastic' about army life, recalled Jeremiah Murphy, 'but said it was easier than farming.'[52] Others were guided by 'instinct' or played it safe and waited to see what their leaders were doing.[53] Dinny Daly stated plainly that 'when the officers went one way the men followed them.'[54] Nonetheless, there was also something in what Billy Mullins said about the London talks, which suggests that the final split in Kerry had been unfolding for some time and certainly did not come as a treacherous surprise. 'During and after the Treaty Talks in

London we were still hoping something good might come from them to keep us united', declared Mullins, a statement which, by its very nature, suggests that some form of a split was on the cards long before the final draft of the Treaty was decided upon.[55]

In fact, British messages intercepted by the IRA as early as September 1921 were reporting 'a break in the ranks' and 'the formation of a society called the IRB in opposition to the IRA'.[56] Though it is unclear whether the divide was directly attributable to the Cahill affair, it is still reflective of serious dissatisfaction, for whatever reason, within the Kerry IRA at this time.

The Local Government files of the period throw up a number of interesting alternatives, which are worth a mention if only to shift the focus away from personality issues. One local IRA man was afraid that the real fighting men were being hard done by. 'The slackers and shirkers seem to have it all their own way so far,' he exclaimed, and 'we make no wonder when people say that the conscientious objectors would be just as well paid in the end as those on active service who did all that was possible to achieve freedom.'[57] Eamon Coogan, the Local Government inspector in the area at the time, wrote at length on the extent of bad feeling in the county and warned his superiors that a return to arms was imminent:

> If an iron rule is not maintained and an iron discipline insisted upon, I see nothing but the beginning of anarchy; perhaps some of our warriors in Kerry would wish to set up a Mexico here so that they may be free to continue the noble profession of arms. I need not tell you that I have been hampered in my work as a result.[58]

Nonetheless, what self-respecting republican was going to stand by and watch a man such as Constable Kearney, 'a most vigilant agent of the enemy Government' who 'squelched the Rising in Kerry in 1916', be appointed to a position of authority within the Free State when there were others such as Eugene McDonagh, a strong proponent of the IRA cause, left to fend for themselves?[59] Is it any wonder that the more principled rebel under such circumstances opted against politics and sought a return to arms?

Jeremiah Murphy, however, had a less admirable motive for desiring a return to war. 'We were too young to do any of the fighting during the preceding two years,' he declared, but 'having all passed out twentieth birthdays, it was no longer kids' stuff.' Clearly tired of working their fathers' farms and eager for some action before it was too late, 'we (became) acquainted with the techniques and tried to imitate the older men in the IRA', he wrote.[60]

IRA veterans interviewed by Ernie O'Malley in the late 1930s admitted that the 1922 split had as much to do with personal issues as it had to do with the Treaty itself. Take, for example, 'Free' Murphy who expelled a number of men before the Truce 'for being no good'; Dinny Daly claimed that 'they came back later in the Free State Army'.[61] There are many sources, furthermore, that hint that Paddy Cahill's anti-Treaty stance was founded primarily on the belief that his removal as Brigade O/C was 'the result of a conspiracy' on the part of GHQ.[62] 'Mulcahy got me in the end', was the personalised way that he described his dismissal to Billy Mullins.[63]

'The cause for Cahill's removal given by Headquarters was that they wanted a younger and a more energetic man,' explained Mullins. 'Then Cahill asked Mulcahy his age and asked why he hadn't been replaced by a younger man!' If Cahill had been allowed to remain in position there is every possibility that a confrontation between Cahill's clique and the men at GHQ could have been avoided. The brigade might not have made any significant advancement, but at least relations would not have been as testy with Dublin or with the local men appointed to fill the forcibly vacated positions. For the Kerry leadership, this battle of wills with Dublin was a far greater issue than any struggle for a Republic.

Neither was the Republic a hugely divisive issue for the rank-and-file in Kerry. The three IRA brigades in Kerry were all decisively anti Treaty.[64] According to Con Casey, the 'rift' that occurred was founded in 'personal loyalties between Cahill's men and those who might be called loyal C na G men'. 'Both sides were Republican' and only a few were seen to join the Free State.[65] In fact, the Free State troops were viewed for the most part as outsiders. Statements show that they either 'came' or 'landed' in Fenit and there is little reference to any of them being in the county before that.[66] They were, according to Dan Mulvihill, 'Dublin Guards' or nearly 'all British army',[67] and while there were reports of some local companies in Killorglin and even 'as far as Glencar who went Free State', the active men of the Tan War were reported for the most part to have remained 'staunch.'[68]

The fact that 'very few' of the IRA in Kerry went Free State and yet still remained bitterly antagonistic towards one another appears to confirm beyond reasonable doubt that the settling of old scores took priority over the affairs of state. What else other than local enmity could explain why Cahill and his men, according to Tom MacEllistrim, 'didn't come in to camps or barracks during the Truce?'[69] Even when they did come in, rumour has it that they chose to occupy separate buildings rather than submit to taking orders from new commandants.[70] Jeremiah Murphy hinted at the levels of resentment that existed between rival groups in the county when he wrote of the controversial elections during the summer of 1921. 'They did not produce the good feelings expected of them,' he reflected. 'Therein lay some of the seeds of animosity and opposition which were taken advantage of later on.'[71]

In sum, the good of the nation was not foremost in the minds of the Kerry rebels, who tended to consider pride more important than principle. Certainly the plight of the ordinary man, such as Tomas Ó Crohan on the Great Blasket Island who longed in July 1921 'maybe (for) some trade if life were settled',[72] did not feature at all in the overall scheme of things. The general view held was that 'the devil (should) sweep' the warring factions 'on all sides'. After all, claimed Ó Crohan, 'don't they say that the Treaty they brought back was wonderful, and, by the devil, if it was, what robbed them of their senses so that some would accept it and some would not?'[73] If this was the feedback from an area which had seen little action apart from a couple of men on the run 'east to the quay',[74] then what was the reaction in the areas more directly affected by the conflict? 'It is a diabolically baffling situation when the average Irishman wants peace,' wrote Frederick Palmer from Cork in April 1922. 'The corner-boy type of soldier no longer meets with the hospitality and the favours he enjoyed during his fighting days,' he wrote, and 'the issue is whether the dreamers and corner-boys shall prevail over three-fourths of the people of Ireland.'[75]

Whether the rebels' actions can be attributed primarily to the dispute over the Treaty or to internal matters still remains a grey area, but one thing we can be certain of is that the usual assumptions made on the war and the 1922 split fall far short of the reality and can no longer be taken at face value.

# 8

# CONCLUSION: A VERY DIFFERENT REBEL?

THE BOY soldiers of the Kerry IRA made their own mark during the War of Independence; they were fighting the same enemy as the IRA elsewhere, but they were not always of the same mindset. Personalities and personal agendas often dominated and the county's reputation in the war suffered because of it. The war in Kerry was not a conventional struggle of Tans and selfless Irish patriots fighting for the glory of Ireland. Instead, the evidence shows that for a good part of the war the Kerrymen were badly organised. Nevertheless, it was not necessarily a good thing for Kerry that the Truce came when it did. Throughout the spring and early summer of 1921, the rebels of the county had improved as fighters; their confidence had increased and a more effective leadership had begun to emerge. The case was also the same in Cork.[1]

According to Peter Hart, the Anglo-Irish Treaty found the IRA there larger and better armed and trained than ever before, buoyed up by its experience of power during the Truce and by the expectation of

*Conclusion: A Very Different Rebel?*

inevitable victory.[2]

Joost Augusteijn takes the same view, arguing that despite GHQ's negative assessment of the military campaign at the time of the Truce, 'further escalation was more likely than they thought'.[3] David Fitzpatrick is less certain in his study of the war in County Clare; in his view the IRA had reached 'an impasse' by mid-1921:

> Despite its vast improvement as a fighting force since the days of close-order drilling after Sunday Mass, it was too poorly armed to have much hope of dislodging the enemy from his heavily fortified strongholds. The flying columns had become little more than fragmented bands of armed men intent on defending themselves against all outsiders.[4]

Marie Coleman similarly reckons that for the Longford Volunteers the continuance of an effective campaign against the British would have been a difficult prospect; indeed, she states plainly that the Longford column 'had grown so ineffective' by May 1921 that the possibility of combining it with the Leitrim column was being considered by GHQ.[5]

Comparatively speaking, the Kerrymen shaped up quite well. In July 1921 the county was arguably in a stronger position than it had ever been. In fact, the evidence shows that there was a general improvement in the overall working of the battalions once inadequate officers were replaced, with the Kerry No. 2 and No. 3 brigades, in particular, seen to be putting on the pressure for the first time in the war. Indeed, if the Truce did not occur in July 1921, it could have worked considerably to Kerry's advantage, distracting from and perhaps diffusing the internal feuding that followed the removal of Cahill and his men.

The changes made by GHQ in Kerry led to increased rebel activity in the brigade areas. However, the Dublin command paid dearly for failing to make its presence felt in the county during the early years of the struggle; the independence of local leaders and the self-sufficiency of their units increased as the conflict gained momentum, with many officers becoming less tolerant of intrusions from outside as a direct result. The rift between senior officers in Kerry occurred primarily as a result of GHQ interference. Certainly the Treaty debate was in no way as divisive an issue as the staff reshuffle proved to be.

Nonetheless, confrontations with GHQ were common in every region and were by no means unique just to Kerry. Marie Coleman has indicated that the arrest of prominent officers in County Longford led to bad blood within the IRA there, particularly over the appointment of new men 'to fill the leadership vacuum'.[6] Peter Hart also believes that when it came to politics it was 'the communal networks that counted, not the chain of command ... The boys almost invariably stuck together, obeyed whomever they pleased and often seceded from the organisation altogether'.[7] Interestingly, Hart also notes that when J.J. O'Connell, the IRA's deputy Chief of Staff, toured the 1st Western Division, 'his reports spoke repeatedly of mutinies, "shocking indiscipline", "private spleens and family hates" and the "necessity of developing a national rather than a narrow local outlook".'[8]

The importance of group networks and republican tradition also featured strongly in explaining men's motives to join the republican movement. The motivation to fight extended only to a certain type, however, with the majority left on the fringes and not necessarily looking for a piece of the action. David Fitzpatrick has pointed out

*Conclusion: A Very Different Rebel?*

that revolutionary violence as a rule tended more towards intimidation, raiding or hair-cropping and produced little in the way of bloodshed in most counties.[9] In Clare, for example, the rebels, through no fault of their own, could not spare the time to lie in wait for an ambush having 'hay to save, cows to milk and women to order about'. They were in every sense 'part-time' rebels who fought when they could afford it.[10]

The same mentality existed among rebels in the parishes of Tipperary; many were farm labourers given the option of taking the IRA oath or giving up their jobs.[11] However, many rebels quickly discovered it would not pay to remain in the fight for very long. Indeed, many units lost good fighters because 'there was work to be done'; this was true for Kerry also, and the rebel campaign suffered because the fighting men had families to support and provide for. As Jeremiah Murphy put it: 'the farm work had to be done',[12] and until such time as it was done, the young men of the county had to put the fight for freedom on the long finger.

Leaders also meant a great deal to the Kerryman, unlike other counties where the leadership was not considered as essential. In Cork, according to Hart, operations were 'unauthorised' and executioners frequently 'self-appointed'.[13] David Fitzpatrick does not see the logic in saying a county could outperform its neighbour because of the presence of a few bold leaders: 'Did Longford outdo its neighbours in violence because of a single blacksmith?' he has queried, and 'if three enterprising brothers had been born a few yards south instead of north of the Clare-Limerick border, would Clare like Connaught have rested in slumber deep throughout the revolutionary years?'[14]

Marie Coleman found that in relation to Longford, Fitzpatrick is too dismissive with regard to the importance of good local leadership. Her research concludes, in fact, that when Seán MacEoin, the blacksmith referred to by Fitzpatrick, was taken away from the fight, the north Longford column was 'seriously debilitated', unable to find an adequate replacement.[15] In Kerry, also, the evidence shows that when respected fighters, such as Tom MacEllistrim and Johnny Connors, were forced out of position or sent back to their own areas, planned ambushes frequently had to be abandoned owing to men losing their nerve. The influence of Paddy Cahill among the men of the Kerry No. 1 Brigade has also been strongly linked to the lack of rebel activity in the area during the campaign. Research has found that once he and other ineffective officers were taken out of the picture by GHQ in the early spring of 1921 more capable men in the region were able to get on with the job of prosecuting the war. In some cases, serious fighters, such as MacEllistrim and Connors, effectively renounced brigade control and were operating independently of Cahill, their officers and the brigade at the time of the Truce.

In short, the rebels of Kerry were an uncertain outfit. Those who made the most progress were often the risk-takers, fighting when they liked for who they liked. The rebels' youth was also a feature of the war in Kerry. Patriotism could often be the last thing on the minds of 'mere boys' with a penchant for blackguarding. 'We were,' explained Dan Mulvihill, 'nearly stone mad', 'half crazy', and always 'playing tricks on one another.'[16] Mulvihill and his friends were no different to most other boy rebels active in the Tan War. Fighters with no formal training or experience, it was their vision of freedom that won the independence war.

The comparisons made with other counties gives us some latitude in judging the role of the Kerry rebels in the overall campaign.

*Conclusion: A Very Different Rebel?*

Unfortunately for historians, the number of regional case studies is limited, which means that any assessment is done without the complete picture. Official reports from the period can often be misleading and it is difficult to discover what actually took place. This present study has sought to consider the central arguments of the war in yet another regional context.

The conventional view of the revolution in Kerry is always under review and it is important to continue the examination, to do justice to all sides involved. The experiences of the Anglo-Irish war were many and exceptional. A 'stubborn insistence' on seeing the War of Independence in what D. George Boyce calls 'its conspiratorial setting',[17] where IRA members 'are cast as willing participants in the struggle and invariably emerge as the victors', has done the history of the period no favours. Glorious beginnings are essential for any county's sense of self, but there remains the need for a more critical examination of the period, so that the folklorists' version will not dominate popular perceptions of the rebel war.

# REFERENCES

INTRODUCTION

1. Liam MacGowen, 'Kerry Activities 1920', *The Capuchin Annual*, Capuchin Publications, 1970, p. 306.
2. *Kerryman*, 5 March 1993.
3. Questionnaire completed by Edward Quirke, February 1998 and now in possesion of the author.
4. Tom Edgeworth, 'Old IRA Days by the Shannon', *The Shannonside Annual*, Vol.1, Asdee: Parish Publication, 1956, p. 46.
5. Kerry's Fighting Story, *Kerryman*, Tralee, 1947, p. 159.
6. Ibid., p.126.
7. Interview with Leo O'Shea, Cahirciveen.
8. J.J. Barrett, *In the Name of the Game*, Dublin Press, Bray, 1997, pp. 31-5.
9. Reverend M.D. Forrest, 'Atrocities in Ireland – What an Australian has seen', Sydney, 1920, *Irish National Association of South Wales*, UCC Pamphlets Collection, p. 804.
10. 'With the IRA in the Fight for Freedom', *Kerryman*, Tralee, 1952, p. 2.
11. Public Records Office London, CO 904/101, RIC County Inspector's (CI) monthly report, Kerry, November1916.
12. Pádraig Ó Loingsigh, *Gobnait Ní Bhruadair, Beathaisnéis*, Coiscéim, Baile Átha Cliath, 1997, pp. 53-54.
13. Lady Edith Gordon, *The Winds of Time*, John Murray, London, 1934, pp. 85-86.
14. Peter Hart, *The IRA and its Enemies: Violence and Community in Cork*

*1916-23*, Clarendon Press, New York and Oxford, 1998, p. 18.

15. Michael Laffan, *The Resurrection of Ireland*, Cambridge university Press, 1999, p.295.

16. Marie Coleman, 'County Longford, 1910-1923: A Regional Study of the Irish Revolution' (Ph.D. dissertation, University College Dublin, 1998), p. 333.

17. Joost Augusteijn, 'The Importance of Being Irish: Ideas and the Volunteers in Mayo and Tipperary', in David Fitzpatrick (ed.), *Revolution? Ireland 1917-23*, Trinity History Workshop, Dublin, 1990, p. 41.

18. Op cit., Coleman, pp. 274-75.

19. Op cit., Hart, pp. 208-210.

20. Peter Hart, 'Class, Community and the Irish Republican Army in Cork, 1917-1923', in Patrick O'Flanagan and Cornelius G. Buttimer (eds.), *Cork – History and Society: Interdisciplinary Essays on the History of an Irish County*, Geography Publications, Dublin, 1993, pp. 974-5.

21. Tom Garvin, *1922: The Birth of Irish Democracy*, Gill and Macmillan, Dublin, 1996, pp. 44-5.

22. David Fitzpatrick, 'The Geography of Irish Nationalism 1910-1921', *Past and Present*, No.78, 1978, p.119.

23. David Fitzpatrick, *Politics and Irish Life 1913-1921: Provincial Experience of War and Revolution*, Gill and Macmillan, Dublin, 1977, p. 227.

24. Charles Townshend, *Political Violence in Ireland*, Clarendon Press, Oxford, 1983, p. 332.

25. Ibid., p. 337.

26. Op cit., Coleman, pp. 195.

27. Op cit., Townshend, pp. 323.

28. Tom Garvin, *The Evolution of Irish Nationalist Politics*, Gill and Macmillan, Dublin, 1981, pp. 122-125.

29. Op cit., Hart, 'Class, Community and the Irish Republican Army in Cork, 1917-1923', pp. 971-72.

*References*

30. Op cit., Fitzpatrick, *Politics and Irish Life*, p. 224.

31. Op cit., Garvin, 'The Evolution of Irish Nationalist Politics', pp. 126-7.

32. Peter Hart, 'The Protestant Experience of Revolution in Southern Ireland', in Richard English and Graham Walker (eds.), *Unionism in Modern Ireland: New Perspectives on Politics and Culture,* Macmillan, Hampshire, 1996, p. 87.

CHAPTER 1

1. Op cit., Lady Edith Gordon, p. 109.

2. Lieutenant-Colonel C.P. Crane, *Memories of a Resident Magistrate, 1880-1920,* Edinburgh, 1938, pp. 184-5, 205.

3. Kerry County Museum (KCM), Con Casey, unpublished memoir.

4. Op cit., Liam MacGowen, 'Kerry Activities 1920', pp. 304-5.

5. Statement made by Thomas Knightley, Killorglin.

6. KCM, Con Casey, unpublished memoir.

7. Op cit., Liam MacGowen, p. 305.

8. KCM Con Casey, unpublished memoir.

9. Op cit., MacGowen, p. 305.

10. Op cit., Lady Edith Gordon, p. 183.

11. PROL, CO 904/115, County Inspector's monthly report, Kerry, May 1921.

12. Ernie O'Malley, *On Another Man's Wound,* Anvil Books, Dublin, 1979), p. 85.

13. 1911 Census of Ireland.

14. Op cit., Crane, p. 205.

15. L.M. Cullen, *An Economic History of Ireland since 1660,* Batsford, London, 1972, pp. 150-158.

16. Thom's Official Directory 1919, Alex Thom and Company Dublin 1919.

17. 1911 Census of Ireland; Thomas Crean, 'Nationalism and Class

Conflict in Kerry, 1914-16' (unpublished dissertation, Trinity College, Dublin), pp. 2-5.
18. Op cit., Cullen, p. 156.
19. Op cit., Cullen, p. 156.
20. PROL, CO 904/107-8, CI monthly report, Kerry, October. 1918 and Inspector General's (IG) report, May 1919.
21. PROL, CO 904/101, CI report, Kerry, November. 1916.
22. PROL, CO 904/103 /107, CI monthly report, Kerry, July 1917, November 1918.
23. PROL, CO 904/108, CI monthly report, Kerry, January 1919.
24. John B. Keane, *Is the Holy Ghost Really a Kerryman?*, Mercier Press, Cork, 1976, p. 26.
25. UCD, Mulcahy Papers, P7/D/2, interview with General Michael Brennan, 1 May 1963.
26. Statement of Dan Mulvihill, in possession of Liam Crowley, Killorglin.
27. National Library of Ireland (NLI), Austin Stack Papers, MS 17,085, letter from Austin Stack to Department of Home Affairs, 27 April 1921 and copy of Land Manifesto signed by Kerry TDs Austin Stack, Fintan Lawlor, Piaras Béaslaí and Seamus Crowley; *Tralee Liberator*, 20 April 1920.
28. PROL, CO 904/115, CI monthly report, Kerry, April 1921.
29. NLI, Stack Papers, MS 17,085, letter from Dr Sheehan, Milltown to General Headquarters (GHQ), 21 April 1920.
30. Ibid.
31. PROL, CO 904/157, report of RIC Intelligence Branch on the Southern District, 28 February 1918.
32. NLI, Collins Papers, P916, A/0485, Kerry No. 2 Brigade to Adjutant-General *c.* May 1920.
33. PROL, CO 904/109, CI monthly report, Kerry, June 1919.
34. PROL, CO 904/107, CI report, Kerry, November 1918.
35. *Kerryman*, 31 January 1919.
36. PROL, CO 904/112, CI monthly report, Kerry, April 1921.

37. Erhard Rumpf and Anthony Hepburn, *Nationalism and Socialism in Twentieth Century Ireland*, Liverpool University Press, Liverpool, 1977), pp. 1-10.

38. PROL, CO 904/95, CI monthly report, Kerry, November 1914.

39. Ernest Blythe, 'Kerry better than Cork in 1915', *An t-Oglach*, Christmas 1962, p. 10.

40. Testimony of RIC County Inspector, Hugh O'Hill, and Sir Morgan O'Connell to Royal Commission of Inquiry, Sinn Féin Rebellion Handbook, Easter 1916, *The Irish Times*, Dublin, pp. 137, 148.

41. *Workers' Republic*, 26 June 1915 cited in Op cit., Thomas Crean 'Nationalism and Class Conflict in Kerry'.

42. KCM, 1994:23, minutes of the weekly meeting of the Tralee Branch of the Kerry Irish Volunteers.

43. KCM, 1994:23, minutes of the weekly meeting of the Tralee Branch of the Kerry Irish Volunteers, 22 March 1915 and 19 April 1915; Op cit., Blythe, p. 4.

44. Testimony of Sir Morgan O'Connell to Royal Commission of Inquiry, Op cit., Sinn Féin Rebellion Handbook, p. 146.

45. Op cit., Blythe, p. 4.

46. Cahirciveen Heritage Centre, statement of Jeremiah O'Connell made to Bureau of Military History, September 1954.

47. Op cit., Blythe, p. 4.

48. Op cit., Crean, p. 7.

49. Tomás Ó Crohan, *Island Cross Talk: Pages from a Diary*, Oxford University Press, Oxford, 1986, p. 28.

50. J.A. Gaughan, *Listowel and its Vicinity*, Kingdom Book, Dublin, 1973, p. 347.

51. Ernest Blythe in Joost Augusteijn, *From Public Defiance to Guerrilla Warfare: The Radicalisation of the Irish Republican Army – A Comparative Analysis 1916-21,* Irish Academic Press, Dublin, 1994, pp. 53-4.

52. Op cit., Blythe, 'Kerry better than Cork in 1915' p. 4.

53. PROL, CO 904/99, IG and Kerry CI monthly report, April 1916.
54. Op cit., Crean, p. 10.
55. Op cit., Blythe, 'Kerry better than Cork in 1915', p. 10.
56. PROL, CO 904/100, CI monthly report, Kerry, April 1916.
57. Op cit., Ó Crohan, *Ireland Cross-Talk*, p. 51; Op cit. MacGowen, 'Kerry Activities 1920', p. 305.
58. *Kerryman*, 3 June 1916.
59. PROL, CO 904/103-104, CI monthly reports, Kerry, October. 1915, April 1916.
60. Testimony of Hugh O'Hill to Royal Commission of Inquiry, Op cit. *Sinn Féin Rebellion Handbook*, p. 136.
61. Op cit., *Sinn Féin Rebellion Handbook*, pp. 136-7.
62. Op cit., Augusteijn, pp. 25-31.
63. Billy Mullins, *Memoirs of Billy Mullins, Veteran of Ireland's War of Independence*, Kenno Ltd., Tralee, 1983, p. 28.
64. UCD, Mulcahy Papers, P7/D/1, Richard Mulcahy on the role of the Irish Republican Brotherhood (IRB); NLI, P913, A/0171, D. O'Sullivan, Officer in Command (O/C), D Company, Tralee Battalion to Director, 2nd Bureau, Dept. of Defence, 14 April 1934.
65. May Dálaigh cited in U. MacEoin (ed.), *Survivors*, Argenta, Dublin, 1980, p. 363.
66. Jeremiah Murphy, *When Youth was Mine: A Memoir of Kerry 1902-1925,* Mentor Press, Dublin, 1998, pp. 86-9.
67. Op cit., Lady Edith Gordon, p. 156.
68. Ibid., p. 133,
69. Ibid., p. 173.
70. Statement of Dan Mulvihill.

CHAPTER 2

1. T.M. O'Donovan, *History of East Kerry*, Talbot Prtess, Dublin, 1931, pp. 104-7.

*References*

2. PROL, WO35 69, summary of reports issued by GHQ Home Forces up to 4pm on 28 April 1916.

3. PROL, CO 904/100-101, CI monthly reports, Kerry, April 1916, September 1916.

4. Op cit., Ernest Blythe cited in Joost Augusteijn, *From Public Defiance to Guerrilla Warfare*, pp. 53-4.

5. Questionnaire completed by Edward Quirke, (February 1998) and in possession of author.

6. Op cit., Murphy, *When Youth was Mine*, p. 86.

7. *Kerryman*, 20 May 1916.

8. PROL CO 904/101, CI monthly report, Kerry, November 1916.

9. PROL, CO 904/100, CI monthly report, Kerry, June 1916.

10. PROL, CO 904/101, CI monthly reports, Kerry, November 1916.

11. Kerry County Library (KCL), P6/2, letter from Thomas Ashe to Minnie Ó Priosun, *c.* 1916.

12. *Tralee Liberator*, 16 August 1916.

13. Op cit., Lady Edith Gordon, p. 109;

14. PROL, CO 904/101, CI monthly report, Kerry, November 1916.

15. PROL, WO35/69, F.P.S. Taylor, Dublin Castle to RIC County Inspector Hugh O'Hill, 12 October 1916; PROL, CO 904/101, CI monthly report, Kerry, September 1916.

16. KCL, Con Casey, 'The RIC Barracks in Tralee – Memories of Seventy Years Ago in Tralee' (unpublished article).

17. Op cit., C.P. Crane, p. 200.

18. Densie Collins, 'Black and Tan Days in Ballydonoghue', *Ballydonoghue Parish Magazine*, 1991; Constable Dunne cited in John D. Brewer, *The Royal Irish Constabulary: An Oral History,* Institute of Irish Studies, Belfast, 1990), p. 67.

19. Op cit., Brewer, p. 77.

20. Op cit., KCL, Casey, 'The RIC Barracks in Tralee'.

21. Op cit., Brewer, p. 67.

22. PROL, CO 904/104, CI monthly report, Kerry, November 1917.
23. Op cit., Brewer, p. 77.
24. PROL, CO 904/103, CI monthly report, Kerry, June 1917.
25. PROL, CO 904/104, CI report, Kerry, November 1917.
26. Op cit., Collins, 'Black and Tan Days in Ballydonoghue'.
27. Liam MacGowen, 'Kerry Activities, 1920', p. 305.
28. PROL, CO 904/101/104/107, CI monthly reports, Kerry, December 1916, December 1917, December 1918.
29. A mythological hero, reputed to be part of Fionn MacCumhaill's Fianna Band.
30. Peig Sayers, *An Old Woman's Reflections*, Oxford university Press, Oxford, 1978, p. 119.
31. UCD, Mulcahy Papers, P7/D/1, Frank Gallagher on the funeral of Thomas Ashe, September 1917; PROL, CO904/104, CI monthly report, Kerry, September 1917.
32. UCD, O'Malley Papers, P17b/102, interview with Tom MacEllistrim; PROL, CO 904/104, comparison of IRA membership returns in CI monthly reports, Kerry, October 1917, December 1917.
33. PROL, CO904/103, IG and CI monthly report, Kerry, July 1917.
34. *Killarney Echo*, 19 October 1918.
35. *Killarney Echo*, 17 September 1918.
36. KCM, 1994:22, letter from Patrick Cahill, Wakefield Prison to Jerry O'Looney *c.* 1916;
37. *Killarney Echo*, 12 October 1918.
38. .*Killarney Echo*, 24 August 1918.
39. PROL, CO 904/104, IG monthly report, December 1917.
40. PROL, CO 904/104/107, Sinn Féin and Irish Volunteer Membership Returns in CI report, Kerry, August 1917, November 1918.
41. Statement of Con Brosnan, in possession of Dr Jim Brosnan, Dingle.
42. PROL, CO 904/105, CI monthly report, Kerry, March 1918.
43. PROL, CO 904/110/113, comparison of Sinn Féin and Irish Volunteer

membership returns in CI reports, Kerry, October 1919, December 1920.
44. PROL, CO 904/108-115, Cumann na mBan membership returns in CI reports, Kerry, January 1919-June 1921.
45. Peter Hart, 'Class, Community and the Irish Republican Army in Cork, 1917-1923'.
46. PROL, CO 904/106, CI report, Kerry, June 1918.
47. T. Ryle Dwyer, 'The MacEllistrim Secrets', *Kerryman*, 19 August 1994. This three-part series compiled by Ryle Dwyer for the *Kerryman* was based on statements made by Tom MacEllistrim in 1951 to the Bureau of Military History.
48. UCC, Pamphlets Collection, P636, Richardson Evans, 'The Anti-Conscription Movement: A letter to an Irish Catholic Bishop' Enniskillen, 1918.
49. KCM, 1995:1, letter from Austin Stack, Belfast Jail to N., 23 May 1918.
50. Op cit., Lady Edith Gordon, pp. 132. According to the *Killarney Echo*, 28 September 1918, a Spiritual Defence Fund was organised by the Convent of Mercy in Killarney which sent out an appeal for 'a million of Rosaries against Conscription' in order to 'build up a spiritual wall of defence around (their) beloved country'. The Tralee Temperance Society had, by that stage, already submitted 8,624 rosaries.
51. Ibid., p. 137.
52. PROL, CO 904/157, report of RIC Intelligence Branch on the Southern District, 31 January 1918 and 30 June 1918.
53. *Killarney Echo*, 1 June 1918.
54. *Killarney Echo*, 1, June 1918.
55. UCD, Mulcahy Papers, P7/A/34, unsigned letter from Causeway to Minister for Home Affairs, 7/10/21.
56. *The Liberator*, 15, June 1920.
57. PROL, CO 904/105, CI report, Kerry, February. 1918.
58. PROL, CO904/157, report of RIC Intelligence Branch on the

Southern District, 30 June 1918.
59. PROL, CO 904/106, CI report, Kerry, June 1918.
60. Op cit., Gordon, p. 134.
61. Op cit., Crane, p. 240.
62. Statement of Con Brosnan.
63. PROL, CO 904/105, see CI monthly report, Kerry, February 1918 and Crime Special on the Return of Cases for Listowel reported to the Competent Military Authority (CMA) under Defence of Realm Regulations (DORA) in the same report.
64. PROL, CO 904/105, CI monthly report, Kerry, March 1918.
65. *Kerryman*, 22 January 1919.
66. PROL, CO 904/157, report of RIC Intelligence Branch on Southern District, 30 April 1918.
67. UCD, Mulcahy Papers, P7/A/31, letter from O/C Kerry No. 2 Brigade to Adjutant 1st Southern Division regarding intercepted letter of Patrick O'Shea, Killorglin businessman, 26 October 1921.
68. PROL, CO904/106, CI monthly report, Kerry, May 1918.
69. PROL, CO 904/114/109, CI monthly report, Kerry, February 1921, August 1919.
70. Percentages calculated from a comparison of the 1911 Census Returns for the Rathmore district with 70 Volunteers named as members of Rathmore E. Company, Fifth Battalion, in *Sliabh Luachra*, vol. 1, no. 2, November 1983; KCL, Op cit., Casey, 'The RIC Barracks in Tralee'.
71. PROL, CO 904/106, CI report, Kerry, May 1918.
72. Op cit., Jeremiah Murphy, p. 105.
73. Op cit., Lady Edith Gordon, p. 156.
74. Op cit., Peter Hart, *The IRA and its Enemies:* pp. 168-70.
75. Ibid., Hart, p. 669.
76. Ibid.
77. Op cit., Jeremiah Murphy, p. 85.
78. *Killarney Echo*, 12 April 1919.

79. PROL, CO 904/115, CI monthly report, Kerry, May 1921.
80. May Dálaigh cited in Op cit., MacEoin, p. 363.

CHAPTER 3
1. *New York Evening Post*, 7 April 1922.
2. C.H. Bretherton, *The Real Ireland*, A.C. Black, London, 1925, pp. 9-16, 80. Bretherton was special correspondent in Ireland for the *Morning Post* and the *Philadelphia Public Leader*. His book was withdrawn shortly after publication due to threatened lawsuits.
3. Ibid., p. 80.
4. Sir Nevil Macready, *Annals of an Active Life*, 2 vols=, Hutchinson, London, 1928, pp. 460.
5. Ibid., p. 524.
6. Op cit., Bretherton, p. 36; Op cit., Liam MacGowen, p. 307; PROL, CO 904/101/102/103, County Inspector's (CI) monthly report, Kerry, November 1916, November 1917, and Inspector General's (IG) monthly report, June 1917.
7. Statement of Dan Mulvihill, in possession of Liam Crowley, Killorglin.
8. UCD, Mulcahy Papers, P7/A/31, intercepted letter from Patrick O'Shea, Killorglin, *c.* November. 1921.
9. Op cit,. Crane, p. 241.
10. Op cit., Hart, pp. 135-41.
11. Op cit., Macready, p. 520.
12. Ibid., p. 534.
13. UCD, Mulcahy Papers, P7/A/22, letter from Director of Intelligence to Chief of Staff, 26 July 1921. By October 1920, GHQ had issued instructions to regard all strangers as suspect: 'Tramps and Tinkers' were considered to be a particular 'nuisance' and 'a useful source of information to the enemy'; see Peter Hart, 'Class, Community and the Irish Republican Army in Cork, 1917-1923', p. 969.
14. *Tralee Liberator*, 15 June 1920; see also 'Tramps cleared by Volunteers

in Kenmare', *Tralee Liberator*, 19 June 1920.

15. Op cit., Lady Edith Gordon, pp. 179-183.

16. Ibid., p. 135.

17. PROL, CO 904/108-109, CI monthly report, Kerry, March 1918, June 1918.

18. UCD, O'Malley Papers, P17b/102, interview with Billy Mullins; May Dálaigh cited in Op cit. MacEoin, p. 364.

19. Op cit., KCM, Con Casey, unpublished memoir.

20. Op cit., Lady Edith Gordon, p. 173; NLI, Florence O'Donoghue Papers, MS 31,176, Florence O'Donoghue to *a chara dhílis*, 9 May 1921.

21. Brian O'Grady, 'Where Eddie Carmody Died', *The Shannonside Annual*, vol. 5, 1960, p. 30.

22. NLI, Florence O'Donoghue Papers, MS 31,176, Florence O'Donoghue to *a chara dhílis*, 5 May and 9 May 1921.

23. Dan Mulvihill statement in possession of Liam Crowley, Killorglin.

24. Con Casey cited in Op cit., MacEoin, p. 372; UCD, O'Malley Papers, P17b/139, interview with John Joe Rice.

25. *Killarney Echo*, quotes taken from editions on 3 August 1918, 28 September 1918, 16 November 1918.

26. *Tralee Liberator*, 17 July 1920.

27. *Kerryman* 24 July 1920.

28. Op cit., Lady Edith Gordon, p. 135.

29. UCC, Pamphlets Collection, p. 804, Op cit., Rev M.D. Forrest, p. 8.

30. *Kerryman*, 31 July 1920.

31. UCD, Mulcahy Papers, P7/A/23, letter from Arthur Vincent to Richard Mulcahy, 30/8/21.

32. Statement of Dan Mulvihill.

33. UCD, Mulcahy Papers, P7/A/24, letter from Fr M.J. McDonnell to Chief of Staff, 22/8/21.

34. UCD, Mulcahy Papers, P7/A/21, letter from Rev Fr D., Causeway, to O/C Ardfert Batt., Kerry No. 1 Brigade, 10/7/21.

*References*

35. UCD, Mulcahy Papers, P7/A/28, letter from O/C 1st Southern Division to Chief of Staff on the state of the Kerry No. 1 Brigade, 5/10/21.
36. Ibid.
37. UCD, Mulcahy Papers, P7/A/34, unsigned letter from Causeway to Minister for Home Affairs, 7/10/21.
38. UCD, Mulcahy Papers, P7/A/3, letter from solicitor J.D. O'Connell, Tralee to Minister for Home Affairs, 22/9/21.
39. NLI, Collins Papers, P916, A/0494, letter from Adjutant General to O/C Kerry No. 1 Brigade, *c.* May 1920.
40. UCD, Mulcahy Papers, P7/A/24, letter from Fr M.J. McDonnell, Ballymacelligott to Chief of Staff, 22/8/21.
41. UCD, Mulcahy Papers, P7/A/24, Kerry No. 2 Brigade to O/C 1st Southern Division, 17/9/21.
42. UCD, Mulcahy Papers, P7/A/28, O/C 1st Southern Division to Chief of Staff, 5/10/21.
43. UCD, O'Malley Papers, P17b/102, interview with Bertie Scully.
44. UCD, Mulcahy Papers, P7/A/28, O/C 1st Southern Division to Chief of Staff re. Kerry No. 1 Brigade, 5/10/21.
45. UCD, Mulcahy Papers, P7/A/20, copy report on the state of the Kerry No. 1 Brigade, GHQ inspecting office, 23/6/21.
46. Tim Pat Coogan, *Michael Collins*, Arrow Books, London, 1991, p. 206.
47. UCD, Mulcahy Papers, P7/A/20, copy report on the state of the Kerry No. 1 Brigade, GHQ Inspecting Office, 23/6/21.
48. UCD, O'Malley Papers, P17b/139,102, interviews with Johnny Connors and Bertie Scully.
49. UCD, Mulcahy Papers, P7/A/35, letter from P. Ó Bugonsaí P.P., Castleisland, 12/12/21; also statement of Edmund Griffin, Castleisland.
50. UCD, Mulcahy Papers, P7/A/34, statement of Michael Doody, Parish Justice, Knocknagoshel; UCD, Mulcahy Papers, P7/A/34, statements of Thomas Begley and his son Thomas Jr, Knocknagoshel.
51. NLI, Collins Papers, P916, A/0495, letter from Tomas Ó Dálaigh,

O/C Listry Battalion, Kerry No. 2 Brigade to Adjutant General, 14 June 1920.
52. NLI, Collins Papers, P916, A/0495, Adjutant General to O/C Listry Battalion, Kerry No. 2 Brigade, 17 June 1920.
53. Op cit., Jeremiah Murphy, p. 195.
54. UCD, Mulcahy Papers, P7/A/36, Adjutant-General to O/C 1st Southern Division, 18/11/21.
55. UCD, Mulcahy Papers, P7/A/24, Chief of Staff to O/C 1st Southern Division, 22/9/21.
56. UCD, Mulcahy Papers, P7/A/36, letter from Martin F. Deely, Brosna, to President de Valera, 14 November 1921.
57. Sr Philomena McCarthy, *Kenmare and its Storied Glen*, privately published, Killarney, 1995, p. 149.
58. UCD, O'Malley Papers, P17b/139, interview with Johnny Connors.
59. *Tralee Liberator*, 13 January 1920.
60. Op cit., Lady Edith Gordon, p. 197.
61. NLI, Florence O'Donoghue Papers, MS 31,207/3, No. 1 Battalion (Castleisland), Kerry No. 2 Brigade to O/C Kerry No. 2 Brigade re. Statement of Castleisland Auctioneers, 15/9/21.
62. Op cit., Gordon, p. 197.
63. Sinn Féin Publicity Department, *The Good old IRA, Tan War Operations*, Dublin, November 1985, p. 45.
64. Brian O'Grady, 'Old IRA days in Ballylongford', *The Shannonside Annual*, Vol. 4, 1959, p. 35.
65. Con Casey cited in MacEoin, *Survivors*, p. 370.
66. PROL, CO 904/112, CI monthly report, Kerry, June 1920.
67. UCD, O'Malley Papers, P17b/102, interview with Tom MacEllistrim; information on mid-Kerry from Michael C. O'Shea, Cahirciveen.
68. Op cit., O'Donovan, p. 107.
69. KCM, Con Casey, unpublished memoir.
70. Questionnaire completed by Edward Quirke, in possession of author.

*References*

71. PROL, CO 904/109, CI monthly report, Kerry, Aug. 1919.

72. PROL, CO 904/107, CI monthly report, Kerry, October. 1918.

73. This sample was composed of Volunteers arrested during 1918-21. Names and backgrounds were taken from local newspapers including *The Kerryman* and *Killarney Echo*, brief particulars of reports to the CMA re. Infringement of the Defence of the Realm Regulations in PROL, CO 904/103-12, Kerry CI monthly reports and numerous other statements and accounts from the period.

74. UCD, Mulcahy Papers, P7/A/20, copy report on Kerry No. 1 Brigade, HQ Inspecting Office, 23/6/21.

75. John Joe Sheehy cited in MacEoin, p. 354.

76. Cahirciveen Heritage Centre, Jeremiah O'Connell statement to Bureau of Military History, September 1954.

77. UCD, Mulcahy Papers, P7/A/20, copy report on Kerry No. 1 Brigade, HQ Inspecting Office, 23/6/21.

78. KCL, letter from Thomas Ashe, Mountjoy Prison to his father, 10 September 1917, where he writes of the 'ordinary' nature of his sentence: 'One year hard labour means nothing more than an ordinary sentence.' Also KCL, letter from Austin Stack, 9 October 1917, on death of Ashe:'God grant that I may meet my fate as bravely and in the same good cause.'

79. Con Casey cited in Op cit., MacEoin, p. 370.

80. A.T. Culloty, *Ballydesmond: A Rural Parish in its Historical Setting*, ELO, Dublin, 1986, p. 237.

81. Statements of Edward Quirke and Dan Mulvihill.

82. Op cit., O'Grady, 'IRA Days in Ballylongford'.

83. UCD, Mulcahy Papers, P7/A/20, copy report on the Kerry No. 1 Brigade, HQ Inspecting Office, 23/6/21.

84. KCM, 1993:52, Christopher O'Grady diary, 21 November. 1921.

85. Ibid., 29 November 1921.

86. PROL, CO 904/110, CI monthly report, Kerry, September 1919.

87. Op cit., Densie Collins, 'Black and Tan Days in Ballydonoghue', p. 89;

Op cit. Gordon, p. 135.
88. UCD, O'Malley Papers, P17b/102, interview with Billy Mullins; P7/A/20, copy report on the Kerry No. 1 Brigade, HQ Inspecting Office, 23/6/21, for impression of Kerry Volunteers as a 'mob'.

CHAPTER 4

1. PROI, CO 904/115, RIC CI, monthly report, Kerry, June 1921.
2. PROL, CO 904/112, CI monthly report, Kerry, July 1920.
3. NLI, Florence O'Donoghue Papers, MS 31,231/1, report of the Enemy Intelligence Officer, 2nd Battalion Loyal Regiment for the period ended 24/11/21; See also PROL, CO 904/153, report of P. Hannon re. kidnapping and robbery, 30 November 1921.
4. PROL, CO 904/153, report of Head Constable, M. Daught, 8 December 1921.
5. UCD, O'Malley Papers, P17b/102, interview with Johnny Connors.
6. PROL, CO 904/153, CI report re. IRA in Cahirciveen, 22 September 1921.
7. NLI, Florence O'Donoghue Papers, MS 31,207/3, O/C No. 1 Battalion (Castleisland), Kerry No. 2 Brigade to O/C Kerry No. 2 Brigade re. Statement of Mrs A. Brosnan, 15 September 1921.
8. UCD, O'Malley Papers, P17b/102, interview with John Joe Rice.
9. UCD, Mulcahy Papers, P7/A/35, Denis Lynch to Austin Stack, *c.* December 1921.
10. *Kerryman*, 20, March 1920.
11. *Kerryman*, 24 April 1920.
12. T. Ryle Dwyer, *Tans, Terror and Troubles: Kerry's Real Fighting Story*, Mercier Press, 2001, pp. 189-90.
13. May Dalaigh cited in Op cit., MacEoin, p. 364.
14. UCD, O'Malley Papers, P17b/139, interview with Susie Casey.
15. UCD, O'Malley Papers, P17b/102, interviews with Con Casey and Denis Quill.

*References*

16. National Archives (N.A.), DELG 12/16, letter from John Brassil, Secretary of Ballylongford Farmers' Association to Minister for Local Government, 1 February 1922.
17. KCL, Minute Books of Rural District Council for Dingle, Kenmare, Killarney, Listowel, Tralee, 1920-21.
18. NA, DELG 12/16, report of Kerry Inspector, 12 October 1921.
19. Ibid.; NA, DELG 12/16, letter from Sean Ó Coclaim to Secretary, Kerry County Council, 20 October 1921.
20. NA, DELG 12/16, letter from Donncadh Ó Cuile, N. Kerry District Court to Minister for Local Government, 19 November 1921.
21. UCD, Mulcahy Papers, P7/A/31, Adjutant, 1st Southern Division to Adjutant General, 1 November 1921.
22. UCD, O'Malley Papers, P17b/102, interview with Bertie Scully.
23. Op cit., Bretherton, p. 89.
24. *New York Evening Post*, 11 March 1922.
25. Op cit., Bretherton, p. 2.
26. NLI, Colonel Maurice Moore Papers, MS 10,556/2, letter from Lady Albinia Broderick to Lady Blyes, 22 May 1921.
27. NLI, Colonel Maurice Moore Papers, MS 10,556/2, letter from T. Moloney, including an extract of a letter received from her brother in north Kerry, 28 May 1921.
28. NLI, Florence O'Donoghue Papers, MS 31,204, W.N. to 1st Southern Division *c.* 1921.
29. UCD, Mulcahy Papers, P7/A/36, letter from Bartholomew Dillane, E. House, Cahirciveen to Secretary, Dáil Éireann, 12 December 1921.
30. UCD, Mulcahy Papers, P7/A/36, letter from Patrick Walsh, Emulaghmore, Cahirciveen, autumn 1921.
31. UCD, Mulcahy Papers, P7/A/21, Adjutant, Kerry No. 3 Brigade to O/C 1st Southern Division, 20 May 1921.
32. UCD, Mulcahy Papers, P7/A/21, Headquarters, 1st Southern Division to Chief of Staff, 24 May 1921.

33. Statement of Dan Mulvihill, in possession of Liam Crowley, Killorglin.
34. Ibid.
35. Sheila Humpheries cited in Op cit., MacEoin, p. 341.
36. PROL, CO 904/106, CI monthly report, Kerry, June 1918.
37. UCD, O'Malley Papers, P17b/102, interview with Tom MacEllistrim.
38. UCD, O'Malley Papers, P17b/102, interview with Bertie Scully.
39. Op cit. Hart, p. 152.
40. KCM, 1993:52, Christopher O'Grady Diary, 7 January 1921.
41. May Dalaigh cited in Op cit. MacEoin, p. 367.
42. UCD, Mulcahy Papers, P7/A/20, report on the ambush of a patrol in Castleisland on 10 July 1921 by O/C Kerry No. 2 Brigade, 16 July 1921.
43. UCD, O'Malley Papers, P17b/102, interview with Johnny Connors.
44. Statement of Dan Mulvihill.
45. UCD, O'Malley Papers, P17b/102, 132, interviews with Bertie Scully, Tom O'Connor and Tom MacEllistrim.
46. Op cit,. O'Malley, p. 144.
47. UCD, Mulcahy Papers, P7/A/31, O/C Kerry No. 2 Brigade to Adjutant, 1st Southern Division, 26 October 1921.
48. Cahirciveen Heritage Centre, statement of Jeremiah O'Connell made to the Bureau of Military History, September 1954, regarding threats of dismissal.
49. Op cit., Barrett, p. 168.
50. PROL, CO 904/109, CI monthly report, Kerry, May 1919.
51. PROL, CO 904/108, CI monthly report, April 1919.
52. Op cit., Augusteijn, p. 26.
53. PROL, CO 904/107-153, CI monthly reports 1918-21.
54. UCD, O'Malley Papers, P17b/102, interview with John Joe Rice.
55. John Joe Sheehy cited in MacEoin, *Survivors*, p. 357.
56. Op cit., Billy Mullins; see also Op cit., Murphy, Appendix III, 'A Grandchild's Eulogy': 'He loved God and his Church'; also UCD, O' Malley Papers, p. 17b/102, interview with John Joe Rice and the earlier ref-

erence to men who were 'particular about duties and going to receive'.
57. Op cit., Mullins, p. 185; NLI, MS 21,697, letter from Lord Justice O'Connor to Cardinal Logue, 21 December 1920.
58. Statement of Con Brosnan, in possession of Dr Jim Brosnana, Dingle.
59. UCD, O'Malley Papers, p. 17b/102, interview with John Joe Rice.
60. UCD, Mulcahy Papers, P7/A/24, Kerry No. 2 Brigade to O/C 1st Southern Division, 17 September 1921.
61. Op cit., Mullins, p. 169.
62. O'Malley Papers, p. 17b/102, interview with John Joe Rice.
63. NLI, Colonel Maurice Moore Papers, MS 10,556/2, letter from T. Moloney, 28 May 1921.
64. Op cit., Billy Mullins, p. 169.
65. Op cit., O'Grady, 'Old IRA Days in Ballylongford'.
66. NLI, MS 21,697, letter from Cardinal Logue to Lord Justice O'Connor, 23 January 1921.
67. UCD, O'Malley Papers, P17b/102, interview with John Joe Rice.
68. Ibid., John Joe Rice.
69. Op cit., MacGowen, 'Kerry Activities – 1920', 1970.

CHAPTER 5
1. UCD, Mulcahy Papers, P7/A/28, Paddy Cahill, O/C Kerry No. 1 Brigade to Chief of Staff, 20 May 1921.
2. NLI, O'Donoghue Papers, MS 31,176, Florence O'Donoghue to '*A chara dhílis*', 9, 10, 13 May 1921.
3. Statement of Dan Mulvihill in possession of Liam Crowley, Killorglin.
4. Cork Archives Institute, Lankford Papers, U169 C, Captain George Power on the responsibilities undertaken by Liam Lynch as O/C of 1st Southern Division.
5. UCD, Mulcahy Papers, P7/A/37, letter from Chief of Staff to Minister of Defence re. abuses in Kerry No. 1 brigade, 7 October 1921.
6. UCD, O'Malley Papers, P17b/139, interview with Michael Fleming.

7. UCD, O'Malley Papers, P17b/102, interview with John Joe Rice.
8. UCD, Mulcahy Papers, P7/A/28, O/C 1st Southern Division to Chief of Staff regarding Kerry No. 1 Brigade, 5/10/21.
9. UCD, Mulcahy Papers, P7/A/20, copy report on Kerry No. 1 Brigade, HQ Inspecting Office, 23/6/21.
10. UCD, Mulcahy Papers, P7/A/28, O/C 1st Southern Division to Chief of Staff, 5/10/21; UCD, O'Malley Papers, P17b/102, interview with Billy Mullins.
11. UCD, O'Malley Papers, P17b/102, interview with John Joe Rice.
12. UCD, Mulcahy Papers, P7/A/28, O/C 1st Southern Division to Chief of Staff, 5/10/21.
13. UCD, Mulcahy Papers, P7/A/20, copy report on Kerry No. 1 Brigade, HQ Inspecting Office, 23/6/21.
14. UCD, Mulcahy Papers, P7/A/28, O/C 1st Southern Division to Chief of Staff, 6/10/21.
15. UCD, Mulcahy Papers, P7/A/28, O/C 1st Southern Division to Chief of Staff regarding Kerry No. 1 Brigade, 5/10/21.
16. UCD, Mulcahy Papers, P7/A/28, letter from Paddy Cahill, O/C Kerry No. 1 Brigade, to Chief of Staff, 20 May 1921.
17. Ibid.
18. UCD, O'Malley Papers, P17b/102, interviews with John Joe Rice, Dinny Daly.
19. UCD, O'Malley Papers, P17b/102, interview with Denis Quill.
20. UCD, O'Malley Papers, P17b/102, interviews with Tom MacEllistrim, Johnny Connors.
21. UCD, Mulcahy Papers, P7/A/20, copy report on Kerry No. 1 Brigade, HQ Inspecting Office, 23/6/21.
22. UCD, Mulcahy Papers, P7/A/20, copy report on Kerry No. 1 Brigade, HQ Inspecting Office, 23/6/21.
23. UCD, Mulcahy Papers, P7/A/28, letter from Paddy Cahill, O/C Kerry No. 1 Brigade, to Chief of Staff, 20 May 1921.

*References*

24. UCD, Mulcahy Papers, P7/A/20, copy report on Kerry No. 1 Brigade, HQ Inspecting Office, 23/6/21.
25. UCD, O'Malley Papers, P17b/139, interview with Dinny Daly.
26. UCD, Mulcahy Papers, P7/A/19, report of 1st Southern Division regarding Kerry No. 3 month of May activities, 11/6/21. The Cahirciveen Battalion, which was originally attached to the Kerry No. 1 Brigade, became the county's third brigade area in the late spring of 1921 following Liam Lynch's appointment as O/C of the 1st Southern Division.
27. UCD, O'Malley Papers, P17b/139, interview with Dinny Daly.
28. UCD, O'Malley Papers, P17b/102, interview with Bertie Scully.
29. UCD, O'Malley Papers, P17b/102, interview with Dinny Daly.
30. Military Archives (M.A.), Cathal Brugha Barracks, Collins Papers, A/0494, letter from Paddy Cahill, O/C Kerry No.1 Brigade to Adjutant General, 8 May 1920.
31. UCD, Mulcahy Papers, P7/A/19, report of 1st Southern Division regarding Kerry No. 3 month of May activities, 11/6/21.
32. Ibid.
33. UCD, O'Malley Papers, P17b/132, interview with Gregg Ashe.
34. UCD, Mulcahy Papers, P7/A/19, report from Kerry No. 3 Brigade regarding activities for month of May 1921.
35. Ibid.
36. Ibid.
37. UCD, Mulcahy Papers, P7/A/20, Adjutant, Kerry No. 3 Brigade to Adjutant General, 24 May 1921 and diary of activities of Kerry No. 3 brigade for month of June 1921.
38. UCD, Mulcahy Papers, P7/A/19, report of 1st Southern Division on Kerry No. 3 brigade, including communications from M.J. O'Sullivan, solicitor, to Kerry No. 3 officers re. terms for possible ceasefire, 12/6/21.
39. UCD, Mulcahy Papers, P7/A/19, report of 1st Southern Division regarding Kerry No. 3 month of May activities, 11/6/21.
40. UCD, O'Malley Papers, P17b/139, interview with Johnny Connors.

41. May Dalaigh cited in Op cit., U. MacEoin, p. 365.
42. UCD, O'Malley Papers, P17b/102, interview with Tom MacEllistrim.
43. UCD, O'Malley Papers, P17b/102, interview with John Joe Rice.
44. UCD, O'Malley Papers, P17b/132, interview with Tom O'Connor.
45. UCD, O'Malley Papers, P17b/102, interview with Johnny Connors.
46. Information from Martin Moore, Tralee.
47. UCD, Mulcahy Papers, P7/A/20, copy report on Kerry No. 1 Brigade, HQ Inspecting office, 23/6/21.
48. John Joe Sheehy cited in Op cit., MacEoin, p. 354.
49. Op cit., Peter Hart, *The IRA and its Enemies*, pp. 207-9.
50. UCD, O'Malley Papers, P17b/102, interviews with Tom MacEllistrim, Dinny Daly and Bertie Scully; KCM, 1994:22, letter from Paddy Cahill, Wakefield Prison, to Jerry O'Looney, 1916.
51. UCD, O'Malley Papers, P17b/139, interview with Michael Fleming.
52. UCD, O'Malley Papers, P17b/139, interview with Johnny Connors.
53. UCD, O'Malley Papers, P17b/139, interview with Michael Fleming.
54. UCD, Mulcahy Papers, P7/A/28, O/C 1st Southern Division to Chief of Staff, 5/10/21.
55. UCD, O'Malley Papers, P17b/102,139, interviews with Johnny Connors, Tom MacEllistrim and Michael Fleming.
56. UCD, O'Malley Papers, P17b/102, interviews with Denis Quill and Dinny Daly.
57. UCD, O'Malley Papers, P17b/139, interview with Michael Fleming.
58. UCD, O'Malley Papers, P17b/102, interview with Johnny Connors.
59. UCD, Mulcahy Papers, P7/A/37, letter from Chief of Staff to O/C 1st Southern Division regarding sale of Ballycarty Lands at Ballymacelligott, 23/6/21.
60. UCD, O'Malley Papers, P17b/102, interviews with Tom MacEllistrim and Johnny Connors.
61. NA, DELG 12/16, E.C., 'Report Killarney', to Department of Local Government, 12 December 1921. Mexico, during the previous decade, had

been noted for its rebellions and civil war.

62. NA, DELG 12/16, E.C., 'Report Killarney', to Department of Local Government, 12 December 1921.

63. UCD, O'Malley Papers, P17b/102, interview with Billy Mullins.

64. Con Casey cited in Op cit., MacEoin, p. 374; KCM, Con Casey, unpublished memoir; U.C.D., O'Malley Papers, P17b/102, interview with Con Casey.

65. UCD, O'Malley Papers, P17b/102, interviews with John Joe Rice and Denis Quill.

66. UCD, O'Malley Papers, P17b/102, interview with Bertie Scully.

67. UCD, O'Malley Papers, P17b/102, interviews with Billy Mullins and Bertie Scully.

68. UCD, Mulcahy Papers, P7/A/38, letter from Chief of Staff to O/C Kerry No. 2 Brigade regarding Headford Ambush, 16/4/21; UCD, Mulcahy Papers, P7/A/19, HQs 1st Southern Division regarding Ballymacandy Ambush, 11/6/21.

69. UCD, Mulcahy Papers, P7/A/38, letter from Chief of Staff to O/C Kerry No. 2 Brigade regarding Headford Ambush, 16/4/21.

70. PROL, CO 904/114 -115, CI monthly reports, Kerry, April-June 1921.

71. PROL, CO 904/114-115, CI monthly reports, Kerry, January-June 1921.

72. PROL, CO 904/114-115, CI monthly reports, Kerry, April-June 1921.

73. PROL, CO 904/115, CI monthly report, Kerry, May 1921.

74. *Tralee Liberator*, 10 July 1920.

75. *Tralee Liberator*, 8 July 1920.

76. *Tralee Liberator*, 17 June 1920.

77. *Tralee Liberator*, 20 July 1920.

75. NLI, Collins Papers, P916, A/0494, O/C Kerry No. 1 Brigade to Adjutant-General, 8 April 1920, 18 June 1920; see also NLI, Collins Papers, P916, A/0495, O/C Kerry No. 2 Brigade to Adjutant-General, 29 April

1920 and O/C Castleisland Battalion, Kerry No. 2 Brigade, 14 June 1920.

CHAPTER 6

1. UCD, Mulcahy Papers, P7/A/28, letter from Commandant Tadhg Brosnan to O/C 1st Southern Division, 21/11/21.
2. UCD, Mulcahy Papers, P7/A/28, letter from Paddy Cahill, O/C Kerry No. 1 Brigade to Chief of Staff, 20 May 1921.
3. UCD, Mulcahy Papers, P7/A/19, diary of activities of Kerry No. 3 Brigade for month of May 1921.
4. UCD, O'Malley Papers, P17b/102,139, interviews with Johnny Connors and Billy Mullins.
5. UCD, Mulcahy Papers, P7/A/35 O/C Kerry No. 2 to D/Adjutant, 28/11/21.
6. Ibid.
7. *Killarney Echo*, 12 June 1920; *Tralee Liberator*, 24 June 1920; *Kerryman*, 31 July 1920.
8. PROL, CO 904/112, CI monthly report, Kerry, July 1920.
9. PROL, CO 904/113-14, CI monthly reports, Kerry, October 1920-January 1921.
10. PROL, CO 904/104, CI monthly report, Kerry, December 1917.
11. PROL, CO 904/114-115, CI monthly reports, Kerry, February-June 1921.
12. 'The Sack of Tralee' by M. de Marsillac in *Kerryman*, 2-13 November 1920.
13. PROL, CO 904/113, CI monthly report, Kerry, October 1920.
14. PROL, CO 904/113, CI monthly report, Kerry, November 1920.
15. PROL, CO 904/113-15, CI monthly reports, Kerry, October 1920-April 1921.
16. Statement of Dan Mulvihill in possession of Liam Crowley, Killorglin.
17. PROL, CO 904/113, CI monthly report, Kerry, December 1920; see also KCM, Con Casey, unpublished memoir.

## References

18. PROL, CO 904/113, CI monthly report, Kerry, November 1920.
19. Letter from Edward Quirke, December 1997.
20. NLI, MS 21,697, letter from Cardinal Logue to Lord Justice O'Connor, 23 January 1921; Thomas F. O'Sullivan, *Romantic Hidden Kerry* (Tralee, 1931), p. 365.
21. Op cit., Bretherton, p. 29.
22. Op cit., Sayers, p. 120.
23. Ibid., p. 119.
24. Report of the Irish White Cross to 31 August 1922, Lester, Dublin, 1922, pp. 99-100.
25. Op cit., Densie Collins, 'Black and Tan Days in Ballydonoghue', 1991, p. 89.
26. *Report of the Labour Commission to Ireland* (London, 1921). A British Labour Party publication.
27. *The American Commission on Conditions in Ireland: Interim Report* (London, 1921).
28. Brigadier-General J.P. Crozier, Ireland Forever, Cape, London, 1932, pp. 91-93.
29. UCD, O'Malley Papers, P17b/102, interview with Tom MacEllistrim.
30. Pádraig Long, 'Memories of the Black and Tans in Dingle' in the *Kerryman*, 5 April 1996.
31. Ibid.
32. KCM, Con Casey unpublished memoir.
33. Op cit., Brewer, pp. 113-114.
34. KCM, 1993:52, Christopher O'Grady Diary, 25 January 1921.
35. UCD, O'Malley Papers, P17b/102, interviews with Bertie Scully and Dinny Daly.
36. KCM, Con Casey unpublished memoir.
37. KCM, 1993:52, Christopher O'Grady Diary, 9 May 1921.
38. UCD, O'Malley Papers, P17b/102, interview with Billy Mullins.
39. UCD, O'Malley Papers, P17b/102, interview with Tadg Kennedy.

40. NLI, Florence O'Donoghue Papers, MS 31,219/2, report regarding members of RIC serving in IRA Company areas, *c.* November 1921.

41. Statement of Dan Mulvihill.

42. UCD, O'Malley Papers, P17b/102, interviews with Denis Quill and John Joe Rice.

43. UCD, O'Malley Papers, P17b/102, interviews with Billy Mullins, Tom MacEllistrim and Con Casey.

44. KCM, Christopher O'Grady Diary, see entries for 7,9,19 January 1921, 23 March 1921, 19 April 1921.

45. NLI, Colonel Maurice Moore Papers, MS 10,557/4, affidavit of Mary Dowling, 6 December 1920; UCD, Mulcahy Papers, P7b/193, notes from a book belonging to Fr O'Donoghue P.P., Ballymacelligott, beginning on 31 October 1920.

46. Hugh Martin, *Ireland in Insurrection, An Englishman's Record of Fact*, Daniel O'Connor, London, 1921, p. 129.

47. Ibid., pp.122-5, 140.

48. UCD, O'Malley Papers, P17b/139, interview with Johnny Connors.

49. UCD, O'Malley Papers, P17b/102, interview with Denis Quill; NLI, Collins Papers, P916, A/0494, letter from Tomas Ó Clumhain to Headquarters regarding Sergeant Restrick, 31/5/21.

50. Statement of Con Dee, *c.* June 1921, in Op cit., *Kerry's Fighting Story*, p. 166.

51. NLI, Colonel Maurice Moore Papers, MS 10,556/2, letter from Lady Albinia Broderick, Tralee to Lady Blyes, 22 May 1921.

52. NLI, Colonel Maurice Moore Papers, MS 10,556/2, letter from T. Moloney, Newtownsandes, including an extract of a letter received from her brother, 28/5/21.

53. NLI, Christina Doyle Collection, MS 5816, statement of Reverend J.J. O'Sullivan, *c.* May 1921.

54. Ibid.

55. Op cit., Crozier, p. 90.

*References*

56. May Dálaigh cited in Op cit., MacEoin, p. 366.
57. NLI, MS 5816, statement of Reverend J.J O'Sullivan, *c.* May 1921.
58. J.A. Gaughan noted in *Listowel and its Vicinity*, Kingdom Books, Dublin, 1973 that the shooting of Sergeant O'Sullivan was the first time that any of the three men who volunteered to do the job had fired shots with a revolver, p. 381.
59. UCD, Mulcahy Papers, P7/A/20, O/C Kerry No. 2 Brigade to HQ 1st Southern Division regarding ambush of a patrol in Castleisland (on 10 July 1921), 16 July 1921.
60. UCD, Mulcahy Papers, P7/A/20, copy report on Kerry No. 1 Brigade, HQ Inspecting Office, 23/6/21.
61. Ibid.
62. Tom Barry, *The Reality of the Anglo-Irish War 1920-21 in West Cork: Refutations, Corrections and Comments on Liam Deasy's 'Towards Ireland Free'*, Anvil, Tralee, p. 41.
63. NLI, Colonel Maurice Moore Papers, MS 10,558/1, letter from Lady Albinia Broderick, Tralee, to Mr Robinson, White Cross Committee, 19 June 1921.
64. UCD, Mulcahy Papers, P7/A/20, copy report on Kerry No. 1 Brigade, HQ Inspecting Office, 23/6/21.
65. UCD, Mulcahy Papers, P7/A/28, O/C 1st Southern Division to Chief of Staff regarding Kerry No. 1 Brigade, 5/10/21.
66. UCD, Mulcahy Papers, P7/A/20, copy report on Kerry No. 1 Brigade, HQ Inspecting Office, 23/6/21.
67. Statement of Con Brosnan in possession of Dr Jim Brosnan, Dingle.
68. Op cit., Barry, p.41 .

CHAPTER 7
1. Op cit., Bretherton, p. 83.
2. KCM, Con Casey, unpublished memoir.
3. John Joe Sheehy cited in Op cit., MacEoin, p. 357.

4. Pádraig Long, 'Memories of the Black and Tans in Dingle', *Kerryman*, 5 April 1996.

5. Review article by Ryle Dwyer on Christopher O'Grady Diary, *Kerryman*, 8 January 1999.

6. KCM, Con Casey, unpublished memoir.

7. KCM, 1993:52, Christopher O'Grady Diary, see entries 11,13,16 July 1921.

8. Op cit., Gordon, p. 197.

9. KCM, 1993:52, Christopher O'Grady Diary, see entries 23, 28 August 1921, 16 November 1921, 4 December 1921.

10. John Joe Sheehy cited in Op cit., MacEoin, p. 358.

11. UCD, Mulcahy Papers, P7/A/20, report on Dingle IRA in copy report on Kerry No. 1 Brigade, HQ Inspecting Office, 23/6/21; PROL, CO 904/153, County Inspector's (CI) reports, Kerry, regarding breach of Truce at Murraigh, 3/10/21, and IRA at Dingle, 7/10/21.

12. UCD, O'Malley Papers, P17b/102, interview with Tom MacEllistrim; PROL, CO 904/153, CI report, Kerry, regarding Ballymacelligott parade, 24/9/21.

13. PROL, CO 904/153, District Inspector Lancaster to County Inspector, Kerry, regarding parade of Killarney Battalion IRA, 24/9/21.

14. NLI, Florence O'Donoghue Papers, MS 31,216, tables showing IRA and enemy strengths in the three County Kerry brigade areas, *c.* August 1921.

15. Op cit., Jeremiah Murphy, p. 172.

16. Ibid., p. 174.

17. KCM, 1993:52, Christopher O'Grady Diary, 17 July, 10 September 1921.

18. KCM, 1993:52, Christopher O'Grady Diary, 8 January 1922.

19. KCM, 1993:52, parade figures in Christopher O'Grady Diary, 6 November 1921; UCD, Mulcahy Papers, P7/A/20, report on Tralee Battalion from copy report on Kerry No. 1 Brigade, HQ Inspecting Office,

*References*

23/6/21.
20. *An t-Óglach*, 11 November 1921.
21. May Dálaigh cited in Op cit., MacEoin, p. 366.
22. John Joe Sheehy cited in MacEoin, pp. 357-8.
23. PROL, CO 906 19, RIC Inspector General to Dublin Castle regarding disorders in Kerry, April 1920-October 1921.
24. Ibid.
25. NA, DELG 12/16, letter from Tadg Ó Cinneide to Minister for Local Government, 1/5/22.
26. The Irish White Cross was established in Dublin for the relief of distress and hardship suffered by persons as a result of the war. Parish committees were established throughout the country and by August 1922 reports showed there was at least 39 White Cross branches in Kerry. The society claimed to make no political distinction in the distribution of relief and provisions were made for IRA dependants and their families affected by the death or absence of a son or father. The regulations governing the distribution of relief stated clearly, however, that acting members of the IRA or the Volunteers were to be excluded from all provisions made. See Report of the Irish White Cross to 31 August 1922 (Dublin, 1922).
27. NLI, Colonel Maurice Moore Papers, MS 10,558/1, papers regarding regulations governing relief for Irish White Cross.
28. NA DELG 12116 letter from Tadg Ó Cinnéide to Minister for Local Government, 1/5/22.
29. Op cit., Macready, p. 540.
30. NLI, Florence O'Donoghue Papers, MS 31,231/1, report of Enemy I/O, 2nd Battalion Loyal Regiment for period ending 24/11/21.
31. UCD, Mulcahy Papers, P7/A/23, communication from IRA Chief of Police to Chief of Staff, 25 August 1921.
32. UCD, Mulcahy Papers, P7/A/23, communication to Chief of Staff regarding Kerry No. 2 Brigade, 25/8/21.
33. NLI, Florence O'Donoghue Papers, MS 31,207/1, reports on Kerry

No. 2 and No. 3 Brigades to 1st Southern Division, 15/11/21.
34. UCD, Mulcahy Papers, P7/A/23, communications to Chief of Staff regarding excesses in Kerry No. 1 and Kerry No. 2 Brigades, 25/8/21; also, HQs 1st Southern Division to Chief of Staff regarding activities in Kerry Brigades, 23/8/21.
35. NLI, Florence O'Donoghue Papers, MS 31,207/1, reports on Kerry No. 2 and No. 3 Brigades to 1st Southern Division, 15/11/21.
36. UCD, Mulcahy Papers, P7/A/37, communication from Chief of Staff to Minister of Defence regarding abuses in Kerry No. 1 Brigade, 7 October 1921.
37. Ibid.
38. KCM, Con Casey, unpublished memoir.
39. UCD, Mulcahy Papers, P7/A/20, copy report on Kerry No. 1 Brigade, HQ Inspecting Office, 23/6/21.
40. Ibid.
41. Ibid.
42. KCM, Con Casey, unpublished memoir.
43. UCD, O'Malley Papers, P17b/102, interview with Bertie Scully.
44. UCD, Mulcahy Papers, P7/A/20, copy report on Kerry No. 1 Brigade, HQ, Inspecting Office, 23/6/21.
45. UCD, Mulcahy Papers, P7/A/28, communication from Minister of Defence to Chief of Staff regarding Kerry No. 1 Brigade, 21/9/21; see also letter from O/Cs Kerry No. 1 Brigade to Minister of Defence, 22/10/21.
46. Murphy had, by the autumn of 1921, replaced Andy Cooney as commandant of the Kerry No. 1 Brigade. Cooney had been forced to retire from the position owing to illness. Murphy's own battalion at Castleisland was officially transferred to the Kerry No. 1 Brigade around the same time to increase his footing in the area. (See KCM, Casey, unpublished memoir)
47. UCD, Mulcahy Papers, P7/A/28, O/C Kerry No. 1 Brigade to O/C 1st Southern Division, 5/10/21.
48. Ibid.

*References*

49. Op cit., Ó Crohan, p. 134.
50. NLI, Austin Stack Papers, MS 17,095, letter from S. Rae, Castlemaine to A. Stack, 13/3/22.
51. Op cit., Murphy, p. 186.
52. Ibid., p. 190.
53. Review article by Ryle Dwyer on Jeremiah Murphy's *When Youth Was Mine*, Mentor Press, Dublin, 1998, in *Kerryman*, 13 March 1998.
54. UCD, O'Malley Papers, P17b/102, interview with Dinny Daly.
55. Op cit., Mullins, Tralee, 1983, p. 143.
56. NLI, Florence O'Donoghue Papers, MS 31,212, O/C Kerry No. 2 Brigade to I/O 1st Southern Division regarding intelligence received from Castleisland, 27 September 1921.
57. N.A., DELG 12/16, E.C., 'Killarney Report', to Department of Local Government, 12/12/21.
58. Ibid.
59. NLI, Austin Stack Papers, MS 17,081, extract from an unnamed newspaper regarding appointment of Constable Kearney to chair a commission for the formation of a Free State Police Force, *c.* March 1922. Also, see letter from E. McDonagh to Austin Stack, 5/3/22.
60. Op cit., Murphy, p. 183.
61. UCD, O'Malley Papers, P17b/102, interview with Dinny Daly.
62. UCD, Mulcahy Papers, P7/A/20, copy report on Kerry No. 1 Brigade, HQ Inspecting Office, 23/6/21.
63. UCD, O'Malley Papers, P17b/102, interview with Billy Mullins.
64. Op cit., T. Ryle Dwyer, p. 346.
65. UCD, O'Malley Papers, P17b/139, interview with Con Casey.
66. John Joe Sheehy and May Dálaigh both cited in Op cit., MacEoin.
67. Statement of Dan Mulvihill.
68. UCD, O'Malley Papers, P17b/132,139, interviews with Tom Connor and Dinny Daly.
69. UCD, O'Malley Papers, P17b/102, interview with Tom MacEllistrim.

70. Information from Michael Ahern, Killorglin.
71. Op cit., Murphy, p. 169.
72. Op cit., Ó Crohan, p. 168.
73. Ibid., p. 197.
74. Micheal Ó Guiheen, *A Pity Youth Does not Last*, Oxford University Press, Oxford, 1982, pp. 64-5.
75. *New York Evening Post*, 7 April 1922.

CHAPTER 8
1. Op cit., Hart, p. 261.
2. Ibid.
3. Joost Aujusteijn, *From Public Defiance to Guerrilla Warfare: the Experience of Ordinary Volunteers in the Irish War of Independence, 1916-1921* (Dublin, 1996), p.324.
4. Op cit., Fitzpatrick, p. 230.
5. op cit. Coleman, p.223.
6. Ibid., p. 215.
7. op cit. Hart, pp. 214-5.
8. Ibid., p. 219.
9. Op cit., Fitzpatrick, p. 406.
10. Op cit., Fitzpatrick, p. 217.
11. Op cit., Joost Augusteijn, p. 37.
12. Op cit., Murphy, p. 105.
13. Op cit., Hart, p. 100.
14. Op cit., Fitzpatrick, pp. 117-8.
15. Op cit., Coleman, pp. 277-8.
16. Statement of Dan Mulvihill in possession of Liam Crowley, Killorglin.
17. D. George Boyce, '1916, Interpreting the Rising' in D.G. Boyce and Alan O'Day (eds.), *The Making of Modern Irish History: Revisionism and the Revisionist Controversy*, Routledge, London, 1996, p. 170.

# BIBLIOGRAPHY

(I) PRIMARY SOURCES
*1. ARCHIVAL MATERIAL*
CAHIRCIVEEN
Cahirciveen Heritage Centre
Copy of the statement made by Jeremiah O'Connell, O/C Cahirciveen Battalion 1914–19, to Bureau of Military History, September 1954.

CORK
Cork Archives Institute
Lankford Papers
University College Cork
'The British in Ireland: 1914-1921', PROL, CO 904 Papers (microfilm):
RIC Inspector General and County Inspectors' reports
Intelligence Officers' reports, Southern District
Crime Enquiries, RIC Circulars, Breaches of the Truce
Judicial Proceedings and Enquiries
Pamphlets Collection
Manuscripts re. conduct of Black and Tans in Ireland, U96, U118

DUBLIN
Military Archives, Cathal Brugha Barracks
Michael Collins Papers

NATIONAL ARCHIVES
Census of Population (1911)
Dáil Éireann Local Government Files

NATIONAL LIBRARY OF IRELAND
Robert Barton Scrapbooks
George F. Berkeley Papers
F.S. Burke Collection
Michael Collins Papers (Department of Defence Archives)
Michael Collins–Austin Stack Correspondence
Christina Doyle Collection
Flower Papers
Frank Gallagher Papers
Hearn Papers
Monteagle Papers
Colonel Maurice Moore Papers
Lord Justice O'Connor–Cardinal Logue Correspondence
Florence O'Donoghue Papers
Austin Stack Papers
Captured Sinn Féin Correspondence
List of Sinn Féin Comhairle Ceanntair
IRA General Orders

UNIVERSITY COLLEGE DUBLIN
Richard Mulcahy Papers
Ernie O'Malley Papers

KERRY
Kerry County Council
General Minute Book of Kerry County Council, 13 February 1913 to 5 August 1918

*Bibliography*

KERRY COUNTY LIBRARY
Rural District Council Minute Books for Cahirciveen, Dingle, Kenmare, Killarney, Listowel and Tralee, 1918–21
Miscellaneous files on War of Independence in Kerry

KERRY COUNTY MUSEUM
Christopher O'Grady Diary
Irish Volunteer Minute Book for Tralee Branch, 1915–16
Correspondence of Patrick Cahill
Correspondence of Austin Stack

LONDON
Public Record Office
Irish Situation, Southern District, 1916–19, WO35/64
Operations, Circulars and Summaries of reports issued by GHQ Home Forces, WO35/69
Post Office Telegrams re. IRA disorders, April 1920 to May 1921, CO906/19
Press Comments on conduct of troops in Ireland, WO35/205

PRIVATE COLLECTIONS
Dr Jim Brosnan, Dingle, County Kerry
Statement of Con Brosnan to Bureau of Military History
Casey family, Tralee, Co. Kerry
Unpublished memoirs of Con Casey
Liam Crowley, Killorglin, Co. Kerry
Statement of Dan Mulvihill

NEWSPAPERS/PERIODICALS
*Cork Examiner*
*The Irish Times*

*Kerryman*
*Killarney Echo and South Kerry Chronicle*
*An tOglach*
*New York Evening Post*
*Tralee Liberator*

OFFICIAL PUBLICATIONS
The American Commission on Conditions in Ireland: Interim Report (London, 1921)
The Constructive Work of Dáil Éireann, Talbot, Dublin, 1921
Hansard, Parliamentary Debates, 1919–21, House of Commons, London
Report of the Irish White Cross to 31 August 1922, Lester, Dublin, 1922
Report of the Labour Commission to Ireland, Labour Party Publication, London, 1921

CONTEMPORARY PUBLICATIONS
Evans, Richardson, *The Anti-Conscription Movement: A Letter to a Catholic Bishop*, Trimble, Enniskillen, 1918
Forrest, Reverend M.D., *Atrocities in Ireland: What an Australian has Seen* Irish National Association of South Wales, Sydney, 1920
Henry, R.M., *The Evolution of Sinn Féin*, Talbot, Dublin, 1920
I.O. (C.J.C. Street), *The Administration of Ireland, 1920*, Philip Allen, London, 1921
*The Sinn Féin Rebellion Handbook, The Irish Times*, Dublin, 1917
Johnson, Thomas, *A Handbook for Rebels: A Guide to the Successful Defiance of the British Government*, Maunsel, Dublin, 1918
Lawson, Sir Henry, *Rapport sur la Situation en Irlande*, Delegation Irlandaise, Paris, 1920
Martin, Hugh, *Ireland in Insurrection: An Englishman's Record of Fact*, Daniel O'Connor, London, 1921
Street, C.J.C., *Ireland in 1921*, Allen, London, 1922

OTHER PRINTED PRIMARY SOURCES

Brewer, John D. (ed.), *The Royal Irish Constabulary: An Oral History*, Queen's University, Belfast, 1990

Callwell, Sir C.E. (ed.), *Field Marshall Sir Henry Wilson: His Life and Diaries*, vol. 2, Cassell and Company Ltd., London, 1927

Carroll, F.M. (ed.), *The American Commission on Irish Independence, 1919: the Diary, Correspondence and Report*, Irish Manuscripts Commission, Dublin, 1985

Macready, Sir Nevil, *Annals of an Active Life*, 2 volumes, Hutchinson, London, 1928

*Memoirs of Billy Mullins: Veteran of Ireland's War of Independence*, Kenno, Tralee, 1983

Middlemas, Keith (ed.), *Thomas Jones, Whitehall Diary, III, Ireland, 1918–25*, Oxford university Press, London, 1971

Murphy, Jeremiah, *When Youth Was Mine: A Memoir of Kerry, 1902–1925*, Mentor Press, Dublin, 1998

Murphy, Jeremiah, 'Troubled Times – a first hand account of the Bog Road Ambush', *Journal of Cumann Luachra*, vol. 1, no. 1, Cumann Luachra Gneereguilla, June 1982

(II) SECONDARY SOURCES

WORKS OF REFERENCE

Boyce, D. George, and Alan O'Day (eds.), *The Making of Modern Irish History: Revisionism and the Revisionist Controversy*, Routledge, Loondon, 1996

Hayes, Richard (ed.), *Manuscript Sources for the History of Irish Civilisation*, Hall, Boston, 1970

O'Farrell, Padraic, *Who's Who in the Irish War of Independence and Civil War, 1916–23*, Mercier Press, Cork, 1997

Rees, Russell, *Ireland, 1905–1925: Text and Historiography*, vol. 1, Colourpoint, Newtownards, 1998

*Thom's Official Directory*, Alex Thom, Dublin, 1919
Vaughan, W.E., and A.J. Fitzpatrick (eds.), *Irish Historical Statistics: Population, 1821–1971*, Royal Irish Academy, Dublin, 1978

BOOKS, ARTICLES AND DISSERTATIONS
Augusteijn, Joost, *From Public Defiance to Guerrilla Warfare: the Experience of Ordinary Volunteers in the Irish War of Independence, 1916–1921*, Irish Academic Press, Dublin, 1996
Augusteijn, Joost, 'The Importance of Being Irish: Ideas and the Volunteers in Mayo and Tipperary', in David Fitzpatrick (ed.), *Revolution? Ireland 1917–23*, Trinity History Workshop, Dublin, 1990
Barrett, J.J., *In the Name of the Game*, Dublin Press, Bray, 1997
Barry, Tom, *The Reality of the Anglo-Irish War 1920–21 in West Cork: Refutations, Corrections and Comments on Liam Deasy's Towards Ireland Free*, Anvil, Tralee, 1974
Beatty, Bertha, *Kerry Memories*, Channing, Devon, 1939
Bell, J. Bowyer, *The Secret Army: The IRA 1916–1979*, Poolbeg, Dublin, 1997
Benton, Sarah, 'Women Disarmed: The Militarisation of Politics in Ireland, 1913–23', *Feminist Review*, no. 50, summer 1975
Borgonovo, John Miller, 'Informers, Intelligence and the anti-Sinn Féin Society: The Anglo-Irish Conflict in Cork City, 1920–1921' (MA dissertation, University College Cork, 1997)
Bowden, Tom, 'The Irish underground and the War of Independence', *Journal of Contemporary History*, vol. 8, no. 2, April 1973
Bretherton, C.H., *The Real Ireland*, A.C. Black, London, 1925
Browne, Maurice, 'Memories of Listowel', *The Shannonside Annual*, vol. 5 (1960)
Carroll, F.M., 'The American Committee for Relief in Ireland, 1920–22', *Irish Historical Studies*, vol. 23 (1982)
Carroll, F.M., '"All Standards of Human Conduct": The American

Commission on Conditions in Ireland, 1920–21', *Éire-Ireland*, vol. 16 (1981)

Casey, Con, 'The RIC Barracks in Tralee: Memories of Seventy Years Ago', (unpublished article, Kerry County Library)

Casey, J.P., 'The Genesis of the Dáil Courts', *The Irish Jurist*, vol. ix (1974)

Collins, Densie, 'Black and Tan Days in Ballydonoghue', *Ballydonoghue Parish Magazine* (1991)

Coleman, Marie, *County Longford and The Irish Revolution 1910-1923*, Irish Academic Press, Dublin, 2003

Coleman, Marie, 'County Longford, 1910–1923: A Regional Study of the Irish Revolution' (Ph.D. dissertation, University College Dublin, 1998)

Coogan, T.P., *Michael Collins*, Arrow Books, London, 1990

Costello, Francis, 'The Republican courts and the Decline of British Rule in Ireland, 1919–21', *Éire-Ireland*, vol. 25 (1990)

Crane, Lieutenant-Colonel C.P., *Memories of a Resident Magistrate, 1880–1920*, privately published, Edinburgh, 1938

Crean, Thomas, 'From Petrograd to Bruee', in David Fitzpatrick (ed.), *Revolution? Ireland 1917–1923* (Dublin, 1990)

Crean, Thomas, 'Nationalism and Class Conflict in Kerry' (unpublished Ph.D, Trinity College, Dublin)

Crozier, Brigadier-General Frank P., *Ireland Forever*, Cape, London, 1932

Cullen, L.M., *An Economic History of Ireland since 1660*, B.T. Batsford, London, 1972

Culloty, A.T., *Ballydesmond: A Rural Parish in its Historical Setting* (Dublin, 1986)

Dwyer, T. Ryle, *Tans, Terror and Troubles: Kerry's Real Fighting Story 1913-23*, Mercier Press, Cork, 2001

Edgeworth, Tom, 'Old IRA Days by the Shannon', *The Shannonside Annual*, vol. 1 (1956)

Figgis, Darrell, *Recollections of the Irish War* Benn, London, 1927

Fitzpatrick, David, *Politics and Irish Life, 1913–1921: A Provincial*

*Experience of War and Revolution*, Gill and Macmillan, Dublin, 1977

Fitzpatrick, David, 'The Geography of Irish Nationalism', *Past and Present*, no. 78 (1978)

Fitzpatrick, David, 'Militarism in Ireland, 1900–1922', in Thomas Bartlett and Keith Jeffrey (eds.), *A Military History of Ireland*, Cambridge University Press, Cambridge, 1996

Fitzpatrick, David (ed.), *Revolution? Ireland, 1917–1923*, Trinity History Workshop, Dublin, 1990

Foley, Kieran, *The History of Killorglin*, Killorglin History and Folklore Society, Killarney, 1988

Garvin, Tom, *The Evolution of Irish Nationalist Politics*, Gill and Macmillan, Dublin, 1981

Garvin, Tom, *1922: The Birth of Irish Democracy*, Gill and Macmillan, Dublin, 1996

Gaughan, J.A., *Listowel and its Vicinity*, Kingdom Books, Dublin, 1973

Gaughan, J.A., *Memoirs of Constable Jeremiah Mee,* Kingdom Books, Dublin,1975

Gaughan, J.A., *Austin Stack: Portrait of a Separatist* Kingdom Books, Dublin, 1977

Gaughan, J.A., *A Political Odyssey: Thomas O'Donnell, MP for West Kerry 1900–1918*, Kingdom Books, Dublin,

Gordon, Lady Edith, *The Winds of Time*, John Murray, London, 1934

Hart, Peter, *The I.R.A. and its Enemies: Violence and Community in Cork, 1916–1923*, Clarendon Press, Oxford, 1998

Hart, Peter, 'Class, Community and the Irish Republican Army in Cork, 1917–1923', in Patrick O'Flanagan and Cornelius Buttimer (eds.), *Cork – History and Society: Interdisciplinary Essays on the History of an Irish County* Geography Publications, Dublin, 1993

Hart, Peter, 'Youth culture and the Cork IRA', in David Fitzpatrick (ed.), *Revolution? Ireland, 1917–1923*, Trinity History Workshops, Dublin, 1990

Hart, Peter, 'The Protestant Experience of Revolution in Southern Ireland', in Richard English and Graham Walker (eds.), *Unionism in Modern Ireland: New Perspectives on Politics and Culture* (Macmillan Press, London, 1996)

Harvey, A.D., 'Who were the Auxiliaries?', *Historical Journal*, vol. 35 (1992)

Herlihy, Jim, *The Royal Irish Constabulary: A Short History and Genealogical Guide*, Four Courts Press, Dublin, 1997

Histon, Jer, 'Further Recollections of Paddy Drury', in *The Shannonside Annual*, vol. 5 (1960)

Holly, Denis and Josephine, *Tarbert on the Shannon* (Donegal, 1981)

Keane, John B., *Is the Holy Ghost Really a Kerryman?*, Mercier Press, Cork, 1976

*Kerryman* (The), 'With the IRA in he fight for Freedom', *Kerryman*, Tralee, 1952

*Kerry's Fighting Story 1916–1921: Told by the men who made it*, Kerryman, Tralee, 1954)

Kostick, Conor, *Revolution in Ireland: Popular Militancy, 1917–1923*, Pluto Press, London, 1996

Laffan, Michael, *The Resurrection of Ireland*, Cambridge University Press, Cambridge, 1999

Laffan, Michael, 'The Reunification of Sinn Féin', *Irish Historical Studies*, vol. 17 (1971)

Lawlor, S.M., 'Ireland from Truce to Treaty: War or Peace? July–October 1921', *Irish Historical Studies*, vol. 22 (1980)

Lee, J.J., *Ireland, 1912–1985: Politics and Society*, Cambridge University Press, Cambridge, 1989

Lynch, Denis, 'The Years of Ambushes and Round-Ups, 1918-1921', *Journal of Cumann Luachra*, vol.1, no.5 (June 1989)

Macardle, Dorothy, *The Irish Republic*, 4th edition, *Irish Press*, Dublin, 1951

MacCarthaigh, Cristóir, 'Sedition, Agitation and the Troubles', in *Kilgarvin in the Beautiful Valley of the Roughty* (1995) - local publication

MacEoin, Uinseann, *Survivors*, Argenta, Dublin, 1980
MacGowen, Liam, 'Kerry Activities 1920', *The Capuchin Annual*, Capuchin Publishers, Dublin, 1970
McCarthy, Francis, 'Freemasonry in Tralee', *Tralee Miscellany*, vol. 6 (Tralee County Library, undated)
McCarthy, Sister Philomena, *Kenmare and its Storied Glen*, privately published, Killarney, 1995
McDowell, R.B., *Crisis and Decline: The Fate of the Southern Unionists*, Lilliput Press, Dublin, 1997
McKillen, Beth, 'Irish Feminism and Nationalist Separatism', *Éire-Ireland*, vol. 17, no. 4 (1982)
Mitchell, Arthur, *Revolutionary Government in Ireland: Dáil Éireann, 1919–1921*, Gill and Macmillan, Dublin, 1995
Moore, Martin, 'Ballymac and the Fight for Freedom', in *The History of Ballymacelligott and its People*, Ballymacaelligott Active Retirement Association, Tralee, 1997
Murphy, Donie, *The Men of the South*, Inch Publications, Newmarket, 1991
Murphy, Fr Michael G., *The Story of Brosna*, Brosna Local History Committee, Castleisland, 1977
Newsinger, John, '"I bring not Peace but a Sword": The Religious Motif in the Irish War of Independence', *Journal of Contemporary History*, vol. 13, no. 3 (1978)
Ó Céilleachair, Seán, 'Tureengarrive Ambush', *Sliabh Luachra*, vol. 1, no. 2, (November 1983)
Ó Crohan, Tomás, *Island Cross-talk: Pages from a Diary*, Oxford University Press, Oxford, 1986
O'Donovan, Frank (ed.), *Abbeydorney – Our Own Place*, Kinidom Printers, Abbeydorney, 1989
O'Donovan, T.M., *A Popular History of East Kerry*, Talbot Press, Dublin, 1931

*Bibliography*

Ó Gráda, Cormac, *Ireland – A New Economic History, 1780–1939* Clarendon Press, Oxford, 1994

O'Grady, Brian, 'Old IRA Days in Ballylongford', *The Shannonside Annual*, vol. 4 (1959)

O'Grady, Brian, 'Where Eddie Carmody Died', *The Shannonside Annual*, vol. 5 (1960)

Ó Guíheen, Mícheál, *A Pity Youth Does not Last*, Oxford university Press, Oxford, 1982

Ó Loinsigh, Padraig, *Gobnait Ní Bhrúdair – Beatháisneis*, Coiséim, Baile Átha Cliath, 1997

O'Malley, Ernie, *On Another Man's Wound*, Anvil Books, Dublin, 1979

O'Shea, Reverend Kieran, *Castleisland: Church and People,* privately publoshed, Castleisland, 1981

O'Sullivan, Pádraig, 'The Headford Ambush' (unpublished article in possession of the author at Beaufort, Co. Kerry)

O'Sullivan, Thomas F., *Romantic Hidden Kerry*, Kerryman, Tralee, 1931

Rumpf, E, and A.C. Hepburn, *Nationalism and Socialism in Twentieth-Century Ireland*, Liverpool University Press, Liverpool, 1977

Ryan, Meda, *The Real Chief: The Story of Liam Lynch*, Mercier Press, Cork, 1986)

Sayers, Peig, *An Old Woman's Reflections*, Oxford University Press, Oxford, 1962)

Shanahan, Tom, 'John Dowd and the Anglo-Irish War' and 'The Burning of O'Dorney', in Frank O'Donovan (ed.), *Abbeydorney – Our Own Place,* Kingdom Printers, Abbeydorney, 1989

Spillane, Denis, 'Rathmore: E. Company, 5th Battalion', *Sliabh Luachra*, vol. 1, no. 2 (November 1983)

Townshend, Charles, *The British Campaign in Ireland, 1919–1921,* Oxford University Press, Oxford, 1975

Townshend, Charles, *Political Violence in Ireland*, Clarendon Press, Oxford, 1983

Townshend, Charles, 'The Irish Republican Army and the Development of Guerrilla Warfare, 1916–1921', *English Historical Review*, vol. 94 (1979)
Townshend, Charles, 'Military Force and Civil Authority in the United Kingdom, 1914–1921', *Journal of British Studies*, vol. 28, no. 3 (July 1989)
Valiulis, Maryann Gialanella, *Portrait of a Revolutionary: General Richard Mulcahy*, Irish Academic Press, Dublin, 1992
Ward, Margaret, *Unmanageable Revolutionaries: Women and Irish Nationalism*, Pluto Press, London, 1983

# Index

Abbeydorney, 97
Adjutant-General, 93
Agrarian disturbance, 18
Agrarian traditions, 73
Allman, Dan, 86, 92
Ambushing, 84
American Commission, 98-9
Ammunition, lack of, 107
    refusal of, 86
Ancient Order of Hibernians (AOH), 71
Anti-Conscription Fund, 36
    pledge, 36-7
Anti-recruiting campaign, 23
Anti-Treaty, 119-20
An tÓglach, 111
Ardfert Battalion, 47, 60, 105
Ardfert command, 81, 112
Asdee, 66
Ashe, Thomas, 27, 60
    death of, 30, 32
    sister Minnie, 27
Athea, 75
Auxiliary Forces, 95, 97-100, 102-4

Ballinskelligs, 83
Ballyard, 109
Ballybunion, 18, 66
    commandeering, 53
Ballydesmond, 59
Ballydonoghue, 97
    publican, 61

Ballyferriter, 21
Ballylongford Company, 59-60
    Farmers' Association, 66
    rates, 66
    'unholy crowd', 65
Ballymacandy Ambush, 47, 71, 92, 95
Ballymacelligott company, 49, 75, 109
    complaints against IRA, 48, 89
    Creamery Society, 49
    parish priest, 75
    shooting of John Leen, Moss Reidy, 96
    Tans, 101-102
Barracks, attacks on, 70-1
    burning of, 93
Barrett, J.J., 2, 22
Barry, Tom, 107, 109
Begley, Thomas, 51
Belfast Boycott, 48
Belfast Jail, 35
Berkerly, Colonel, 100
Black and Tans, 75, 95, 97-104, 106-7
Blasket Island, 23, 30, 121
Blood sacrifice, 24
Blythe, Ernest, 19, 26
Boycott, Sinn Féin, 36
Boyle, George C., 127
Brassil, John, 66
Brassil, Henry, 27
Breen, Father, 75
Brennan, Michael, 17

Bretherton, C.H., 42, 67, 97, 108
British Armed Forces, 24, 43
British Government, 38, 66
British Officers, 43
Broderick, Lady Albina, 3, 67, 103
Brosna, 1916, 29
    irate writer from, 54
Brosnan, Con, 32, 37, 74, 92, 105, 107
Brosnan, Tadg, 115-6
Brugha, Cathal, 89
Byrne, John, 49

Cahill, Paddy, 50, 65, 78, 81-90, 94
    brigade staff, 80
    influence, 87-9
Cahirciveen, 68, 84, 111
    battalion, 82-83
    ceasefire, 84
    military, 99
    state of crisis, 69
    tyres slashed, 64
Cahirdaniel, 3
    caretaker shot, 64
Carmody, Eddie, 75
Castlecove, 111
Castlegregory Battalion, 64, 115
    Easter 1916, 26
    shooting of Patrick Foley, 64
Castleisland, 86
    auctioneers, 54
    barracks, 70
    battalion, 89
    kidnapping of William Huggard, 46
Castlemaine, 71
Catholics, 9, 46
Catholic tradition, 74
Cattle-driving, 18
Causeway, 48
Christmas 96-7

Civil War, 111
Clare rebels, 4, 6-7, 125
Class difference, 13-14, 70
Clergy, 74-5
    accusations of, 48
Clifford, Thomas, 47
Clonbanin, 92
Coleman, Marie, 5, 123-5
Collins, Densie, 29, 98
Collins, Michael, 9, 52
Commandeering, 53, 68, 111
Connors, Johnny, 51, 54, 64, 71, 85-86, 92, 95, 102, 126
Conscription, 23-4, 32, 35, 37
    Bill, 35
    fear of, 17
Coogan, Eamon, 90, 118
Cooney, Andy, 90, 116
Cordal, 51
Cork, 19, 107
Cork No. 3 Brigade, 113
Coronation, King George, 12
Coughlan, Sergeant, 30
Council rates, 66
County Council, 112
County Jail, 99
Court martial, 110
Crane, Colonel C.P., 11, 28, 37
Cromane, 36
Cronin, Jack, 70
Crown Forces, 51, 75, 95-6, 108
Crozier, F.P., 98, 104
Cumann na mBan, 32-3

Dáil Éireann, 68
    institutions, 2, 8
    Subscription Fund, 28
*Daily News*, 101
Dálaigh, May, 25, 70
Daly, Charlie, 41, 104

*Index*

Daly, Constable, 100
Daly, Dinny, 82-3, 87, 89, 99, 117, 119
Daly, Martin, 55
Daly, Tom, 52-3, 95-6, 104
Dalton, Paddy, 75, 102
Deasy, Liam, 106
Dee, Con, 102
Defence Fund, 35-36
Denny Street, 13
De Valera, President, 54, 59
Dillane, Bartholomew, 68-69
Dillon, family of, 63
Dingle, 21, 108-9
    battalion, 60, 109
    Tans, 98
    Volunteers, 56, 106-7
Divide, between town/country, 70
Dowling, Mary, 101, 111
Doyle, Michael, 80
Duagh, 66
Dublin, 27, 62, 81-2, 86, 120
    Guards, 120
Duffy, Jimmy, 100
Dunne, Constable, 28-29, 99
Dunquin, 21

Easter 1916, 21, 25-6
Easter martyrs, 30
East Lancashire Regiment, 100
Emulaghmore, 68
Evictions, 22

Factionalism, 90
Famine, south Kerry, 69
Farmer's Bridge, 85, 105
Farmers' Vigilance committees, 38
Farranfore, 79
    Rising, 27
Fenianism, 23-24
Fenians, clerical view, 75
    traditions, 73-74
    uprising, 2
Fenit, 110
Fermoy, 89
Field's Bridge, 85
First Southern Division, 49, 78-9
First Western Division, 124
First World War, 32
Fitzgerald, Desmond, 21
Fitzpatrick, David, 5-7, 9, 123-5
Fleming, Michael, 80, 88-89
Flying columns, 91, 105, 107, 123
Flynn, Jack, 71
Foch, General, 12
Foley, Patrick, 64
Food shortages, 69
Forrest, Reverend M.D., 3, 46
Free State, 117, 119-20

Gaelic language, 21
Galway, 63
Garvin, Tom, 5, 8-9
Gaughan, J.A., 10
General Headquarters, 18, 48
    ammunition, 82
    brutal treatment, 102
    Cahill, 87, 119-20
    changes made, 124
    command, 6-7
    communications to, 113
    inefficient officers, 81, 114, 126
    instructions from, 80, 89
    IRA relations, 114
    Kerry IRA, 79
    Kerry No. 1 Brigade, 116-7
    list of arms, 107
    military campaign, 123
    reputation, 52-3, 58
    Volunteer misconduct, 62
German Plot, 39

Glen, The, 83
Glenbeigh, 51, 105, 112
   ambush, 69
Glencar company, 60
   people of, 69
Glenflesk, 110
Glens, 77
Gneevguilla, 110
Gordon, Lady Edith, 11, 13-4, 25, 27, 35, 40, 44
Gortaclea Barracks, 86
Gortnaglanna, 75, 102
Griffin, Edmund, 51
Guerin, Julia, 111

Haig, General, 12
Hart, Peter, 4-5, 9, 40, 70, 87, 122, 124-5
Harty, Father, 76
Headford Ambush, 47, 91
Heard, G.M., 36, 38-39, 73, 96
Heavey, Sergeant, 100
Hickey, Colonel, 18
Hillards, 15
Home Rule, 12, 31
Home Ruler, 4
Hopkins, Head constable, 100
Horgan, Moss, 102
Huggard, William, 46
Humpheries, Sheila, 69

Internment Camps, 72
Irish Parliamentary Party (IPP), 19
Irish Republican Party (IRA)
   abuses, 111
   activity, 95-97
   apathy, 50
   ardent critic of, 67
   camps, 68
   chief of police, 112
   conscription, 96
   enemies of, 62, 64-5
   excesses, 112-113
   fear of, 54
   inappropriate behaviour, 47
   making application to join, 59
   mob practice, 110
   officers, 17, 37
   officials, 81
   priests' attitudes to, 77
   resistance to, 9
   shortcomings, 68
   split, 117
   town based, 74
   types, 44
Irish Republican Brotherhood (IRB), 21-2, 24
   opposition to IRA, 118
Irish Transport and General Workers Union (ITGWU), 73-4
Irish Volunteer
   branches, 19-20
   companies, 19
   membership, 22-24, 32-33
   relationship with Sinn Féin, 31
   Tralee branch, 20, 23

Kavanagh, Seán Óg Mac Murragh, 21
Keane, Fr, 75
Keane, John B., 17
Kearney, Constable, 119
Keel, 95, 105, 117
Kelly, Cornelius, 64
Kenmare, 21, 28, 35, 110-12
   bullock taken in, 64
Kenmare, Lord, 54
Kennedy, J.P., 80
Kennedy, Tim (Tadg), 65, 100, 112
Kennelly, Commandant Thomas, 48
*Kerry's Fighting Story,* 1
*Kerryman,* 93

## Index

Kerry No. 1 Brigade, 65, 70, 78, 80-1, 83, 90, 94, 105, 113, 117, 126
    battalion rolls, 59
    brigade staff, 46, 50
    medical officer, 18
    removal of officers, 81
Kerry No. 2 Brigade, 51, 54, 69-70, 85-6, 89-91, 113, 123, 109-10
    officers, 18
    RIC attitudes to, 100-1
Kerry No. 3 Brigade, 69, 85, 113, 123
Kiely, Fr, 75
Kilcummin, 35, 69
Kilflynn, 48
Kilgarvin, 66, 75
Killarney, 40, 64, 79, 117
    barracks, 100
    battalion, 109-110
    census, 15-16
    hunting, 64
    Rising, 27
    tinkers hunted from, 44
*Killarney Echo*, 31, 35
Killeentierna, 103
Killorglin, 18
    battalion, 105
    rates, 66, 70
    re-establishment of Volunteers, 21
    Rising, 27
    town rebels, 71-2
    Volunteers on the run, 43
    Volunteer theft, 46
Kilmorna House, 55
Kitchener, Lord, 12
Knocknagoshel, 51, 71

Labour Party Commission, 27
Labourers, 16-9, 38
    as Volunteers, 57
Laffan, Michael, 5
Lalor, Sergeant, 102
Land
    acts, 15
    agitation, 17, 37, 73
    hunger, 5
    reform, 14
    wars, 2
Leaders 1916, 1
Leary, Mick, 109
Leen, John, 96
Leitrim, 123
Limerick, 48
Listowel, 56, 59, 63, 66, 81
    census, 15-6
    company, 106
    drill meetings, 38
    Easter 1916, 26
    shooting of Sergeant O'Sullivan, 105
    Volunteer progress, 22
Listry Battalion, 52
Lixnaw, 48
Local Government Files, 118
Logue, Cardinal, 76, 97
*London Illustrated News*, 12
Long, Padraig, 108
Lovett, Maurice, 101
Loyal Regiment, Second Battalion, 63
Lynch, Liam, 48-50, 53, 69, 79-80, 83-4, 106, 114, 116
Lyons, Jerry, 75, 102

MacEllistram, Tom, 56, 69-70, 71-2, 85-7, 89-90, 92, 101, 120, 126
MacEoin, Seán, 7, 126
MacEoin, Uinseann, 104
MacGowen, Liam, 12-13, 23
MacKinnon, Major John, 102, 116
MacNeill, Eoin, 22

MacNeillites, 24
Macready, General Nevil, 43, 71, 79
Macroom, 63
MacSwiney, Terence, 95
Malicious injury claims, 66
Marstall, Archdeacon, 75
Martial Law Proclamation, 93
Martin, Hugh, 101-2
Maunsel, District inspector, 36
Mayo Volunteers, 5
McCarthy, D.M., 51
McCarthy, Sister Philomena, 54
McDonagh, Eugene, 119
McDonnell, Fr, 48, 75
Mexico, 89, 118
Mills bombs, 106
Milltown, 18
Moonlighting, 11, 73-74
Moriarty, Commandeant, 106
Motives for joining Volunteers/Sinn Féin, 58-9
Moynihan, Con, 53
Moynihan, Jamsey, 46
Muckross House, 46-7
Mulcahy, Richard, 47-8, 50, 75, 78, 81, 83, 91, 94, 116, 119
Mullins, Billy, 24, 61, 76, 80, 95, 99, 101, 117-9
Mulvihill, Dan, 17, 25, 43, 46-7, 59, 69, 100, 120, 126
Murphy, Humphrey (Free), 90-91, 93, 116-7, 119
Murphy, Jeremiah, 40, 53, 117, 120, 125

Nationalism, 24
Nationalist feeling, 32
National Volunteers, 19-22
Newtownsandes, 32, 48, 66, 101, 106
*New York Evening Post*, 67

Ní Bhrudair, Gobnait, 3

O'Brian, Padraig, 21
Ó Clumhain, Tomás, 102
O'Connell, Jeremiah, 58
O'Connell, J.J., 124
O'Connell, Sir Morgan, 20
O'Connor, E., 20
O'Connor, John (Killarney), 68
O'Connor, John (Killeentierna), 103
O'Connor, Tom, 86, 91
O'Connor, Tom Scarteen, 54
Ó Crohan, Tomás, 121
O'Donnell, Tom, 71
O'Donoghue, Florence, 45, 66, 78-9, 101
O'Dorney, 102
O'Gerity, E., 14, 56, 91-2
O'Grady, Brian, 45, 59, 60, 76
O'Grady, Christy, 60, 70, 99, 101, 109-10
O'Hill, Hugh, 19, 24, 27
O'Leary, Ellen, 111
O'Leary, Michael, 51
O'Mahony, Brigadier Dan, 86
O'Malley, Ernie, 14, 72, 79, 85, 88, 119
O'Malley, Captain, 99
O'Shea, Patrick, 38, 43
O'Sullivan, Fr James, 87
O'Sullivan, M. J., 84
O'Sullivan, Reverend J.J., 103-4
O'Sullivan, Sergeant, 105, 107
Outrages
    in Sinn Féin's name, 38
    IRA, 91-92, 95

Palmer, Frederick, 67, 121
Patriotism, 126
Population, Kerry, 15-6
Priests, 47, 74, 76-7

*Index*

Quill, Denis, 61, 66, 90, 101-102
Quirke, Edward, 26, 56, 59

Raids, 34, 59, 91, 112
Ranalough, 29
Rate collectors, 66
Rathmore, 68
    battalion, 109
    company, 39
Reardon, Mick, 75
Rebellion, 26, 30, 67
Rebellion Commission, 21, 24
Redmond, John, 19-20, 22, 24
Redmondite campaign, 22-3
Redmondites, 20
Redmondite split, 19
Reidy, Moss, 96
Reprisals, 68, 94, 96, 104
Republic, 1, 69, 120
Republican
    aspirations, 18
    attitudes to Tans, 99
    followers, 72
    land, 14
    mobilising, 13
    motives, 60
    principles, 45
    reluctant, 38
    rhetoric, 23
Republicanism, 18
Restrick, Sergeant, 102
Rice, John Joe, 46, 64, 73, 75, 77, 80, 90-1, 101
Rising 1916, 26, 37, 90, 119
Road cutting, 84, 91
Royal Irish Constabulary (RIC)
    assaults against, 27
    attitudes towards IRA, 43, 45, 56
    friendly, 29, 100
    intelligence branch, 36
    King's, 98
    raids, 70
    rank and file, 29
    Rising 1916, 26
    outrages, 62
    withdrawal from Cahirdaniel, 64

Safe houses, 69
Safekeeping (guns), 85
Sayers, Peig, 30, 97
Scartaglin, 29
Scouts, 71
Scully, Bertie, 51, 71, 83, 116
Sheehan, Doctor, 18
Sheehy, John Joe, 58, 70, 87, 108-109, 111, 114-5
Sinn Féin
    clubs, 36
    collectors, 36
    courts, 66, 76, 92, 111
    defenders of people, 37
    funds, 36
    land grabbing within, 14
    leaders, 27
    membership, 32-33
    movement, 23
    political, 31
    reorganisation of, 29
    resolve, 34
    split, 38
    submarine base, 28
Sinn Féiners, 18, 21
Sliabh Mís, 50
Sneem, 53
Spies, 44, 67
Split 1922, 117, 119
Stack, Austin, 20, 24, 35, 60
Strand Street, 116

Tailors' Club, 56
Tangney, Bill, 3
Tarbert, 66
    Company, 60, 107
Taylor, F.P.S., 28
*The Sphere*, 12
Tinkers, 44
Tipperary rebels, 5, 125
Townshend, Captain, 100
Townshend, Charles, 5-7
Tralee, 68, 70, 72, 79, 86, 114, 116
    battalion, 80, 88, 105
    census, 15
    Easter 1916, 26-7
    - Killorglin road, 95
    landowner kidnapped, 54
    postmaster, 12
    Tans, 102
Treaty, 117-9, 121
Truce, 105, 108-110, 112-3, 116, 120, 122
Trucileer, 111

Unions, 73

Vale, Joe, 85
Valentia Island, 12-13, 30, 56
Vicars, Sir Arthur, 55
Vincent, Arthur, 46-7
Volunteer
    background, 43, 46, 56, 73
    clubs, 31
    development of, 72
    fleecing done by, 72
    irregularities, 49
    misconduct, 5
    mobilising, 26
    moderates, 60
    movement, 17
    rank and file, 34
    relationship with loyalists, 46
    retribution, 64
    sample of occupations, 57
    sedition, 21
    type, 42, 81
    units, 81
Volunteering, 26, 40

Walsh, Paddy, 102
Walsh, Patrick (Emulaghmore), 68-69
Walsh, Patrick (Gortnaglanna), 75
War of Independence, 122
Warden, Colonel, 111
Waterville, 83-84
West Britons, 12
Western Front, 20
Whelan, Constable, 100
White Cross money, 48, 112
*With the IRA in the Fight for Freedom*, 1
Women's international League, 97
Workers' Republic, 20

Young Turks, 38